X

The Story of a Magic Pill

How People Use the Xpill to Get Clarity, Break Through Blocks, and Access the Power of the Unconscious Mind

X: The Story of a Magic Pill

This product is not intended to diagnose, treat, cure, or prevent any disease.

This book is dedicated to everyone who is reaching for the next level.

X: The Story of a Magic Pill

Don't believe a word I'm about to tell you.

Not because it's not true, but because I can't *tell* you the truth. You can only experience it for yourself.

An experience brings you to your own conclusions, and
(perhaps more importantly)
your own questions.

If you want to experience it immediately,
go to Xpill.com.

Foreword, by JJ Virgin

"If only we could make personal development more real, more tangible...."

That's what I said, sitting across from Robbe in the lounge of a New York hotel just after my speech about the Virgin Diet.

Products for health are clearly effective. The Virgin shakes and bars help thousands of people stay healthy and energized. But they only work when someone makes the commitment to their health and then takes action. I was looking for that magic pill that could help them take action.

"I have one," Robbe said. "I'll show you at the next TLC."

TLC is the Transformational Leadership Council, led by Jack Canfield. It's an invitational group of authors and speakers who meet together to take a break, have fun and share our latest discoveries. I knew Robbe as "the Zappos guy." He was culture strategist at Zappos.com, and he wrote *The Culture Blueprint* to help companies become world class organizations.

When he took the stage at TLC in Costa Rica, I didn't know what to expect, but I was totally curious. His story—beginning with the Red Pill scene of *The Matrix*, experimenting at Burning Man and then creating a real pill—had us all hanging on his every word and yet laughing at how ridiculous it all is.

He then did a demonstration of the process on stage, and gave us each the Xpill so we could have our own experience. We gathered in small groups and you could hear laughter and crying and people having deep conversations in a matter of minutes.

One woman used it to "feel the love of God through her husband" and felt butterflies in her stomach all over again. John Grey used it to write his next book, as did several other authors there, and Nicole Brandon used it successfully to get more acting roles. And I used it when I felt stuck and needed a little push to move forward with my next big goal.

And the experience had a total ripple effect. For the rest of the trip you would hear people talking about their Xpill experiences or sitting down and trying it with each other.

I'm always looking for mind-blowing experiences to give to my mastermind clients and to have at my annual Mindshare Summit where the most innovative health and wellness practitioners meet to share what we've learned, so I invited him to speak.

Everyone was blown away, at first by the funny and engaging presentation, and then by their own experience. It's not always what you expect: one woman started off wanting more for her business but had a total breakthrough in love (that has lasted to this day). Another woman's legs were shaking violently as she said, "I feel like I'm releasing trauma after taking the pill." Others used it to commit to their big goals.

It was fun, transformative and we all got to know each other on a much deeper level. I constantly share about the experience, and other events and masterminds are catching on.

What excites me is that the Xpill can work across belief systems, across programs, across techniques. It helps people uncover the deeper issues, make bold commitments, and open up in ways they never have before. The Xpill is nothing, and yet it's everything. It's a pill, and yet it's really you. And in a world where self-development can get so complicated, heavy, and heady, Robbe has made it simple, light, and an experience in the body.

X: The Story of a Magic Pill

If any of this sounds crazy or incredulous, then honestly, I hope you don't believe me. I hope you simply try it for yourself and let your own experience show you what's real.

Contents

Who am I?

This book is not about me. But I realize that people have heard about this and have no idea what to think without knowing who I am. They see the videos and ask, "Who is this guy, some kind of quack?"

So... in order for you to know who's talking to you, here's my professional biography:

Robert Richman is a culture hacker and former Culture Strategist at Zappos. He was the co-creator of *Zappos Insights*, an innovative program focused on educating companies on the secrets behind Zappos's amazing employee culture.

Robert built *Zappos Insights* from a small website to a thriving multimillion dollar business teaching over 25,000 students per year. Through his work, Robert has helped to improve the employee culture at hundreds of companies.

As one of the world's authorities on employee culture, Robert is a sought-after keynote speaker at conferences around the world and has been hired to teach culture in person at companies like Google, Toyota, and Eli Lilly. He has used innovative techniques to build culture, such as bringing improv comedy to the workplace and open-space conference areas for companies to develop their strategies and solve problems.

His book *The Culture Blueprint* is a systematic guide to how a workplace can help people grow, inspire amazing service, and ultimately drive revenue through amazing culture.

Robert graduated from Northwestern University with a degree in film, as well as from Georgetown University's Leadership Coaching Program. He is a member of the Transformational Leadership Council, and is based out of San Diego. He's obsessed with great coffee and The Muppets.

Acknowledgments

Honestly, I don't know whether to call it inspiration, intuition, God, or the Universe; but it's not "me." I am a conduit for a greater message, and I'm so grateful I get to play this part in the theater of life.

I get to play with a whole cast of characters. First, and foremost, Holly McMullin, my venture partner who believed in this and in me, years before anything would happen. There have been many who have believed since the early years — Charles Planck, Robert Bahkshai, Brian Schoenbaum, David and Heather Caren.

Thank you to Maru and the Infinite Receivers for being so open and willing, and to Jack Canfield, Donna Steinhorn, and the Transformational Leadership Council for putting me on stage for the first time. To JJ Virgin for all her magnificent support. To Karl Krummenacher for his fierce coaching. To Vishen Lakhiani and the Afest community. To Scott Coady and the Association of Transformational Leaders. To Lisa Sasevich for her brilliant coaching and willingness to take the Xperience to her mastermind groups. To Mike Koenigs for being one of our best case studies and for helping me publish this book. And to Stewart Emery for his brilliant mentoring.

Thank you to all our beta users and the first in the Xpill Revolution, with a special shout out to Joan Emery, Karolyn McKinley, Kavita Singh, Sandy Steers, and Rachelle Lipford.

Thank you especially to Cassie Bjork, my parents Judy and Rick, Michael J. Liskin, Teri Cochrane, Jolene Brighten, Nicole Willis, Summer Bock, Ann Shippy, and the entire Mindshare Mastermind.

It's blown my mind the way people have used the Xpill.

Rob used it to start his photography business.

Brian used it to finally commit to seeing Japan after dreaming about it for 7 years.

Kavita used the Xpill to help her make choices about moving to a different country.

Sandy used her Xpills to write a screenplay in the Xpill 90 day Revolution group. That screenplay placed in the top 100 screenplays of a major competition.

Amir used the Xpill to leave his life of political consulting and pursue his true passion: music.

Faith used the Xpill to let go of an on-again/off-again relationship and found a new level of love that matched what she'd been asking for.

And here are a few of the posts and messages I've seen on Facebook:

> **Shari Aldrich** The XPill experiment
> Today, 10 of us met on the beach and shared our universal challenge and/or goal for the future. The XPill is an experience - and it is a way to set your intention, get clarity on your vision, and gain accountability.
>
> The 10 of us who shared this experience shared some very profound thoughts and wishes. After sharing the intention, we swallowed our pill - which was a placebo. We then took note of the sensations we were feeling. For me, after sharing my intention, I felt a fluttering in my belly. A few minutes later, I felt a hot, burning sensation in my belly.
>
> Here's the COOL part!!! Seriously, cool.
> I shared my intention and literally within 6 hours, the first manifestation of my vision has come to fruition already.
> 2017 is going to be amazing.
> Like · Reply · 7 · 20 hrs

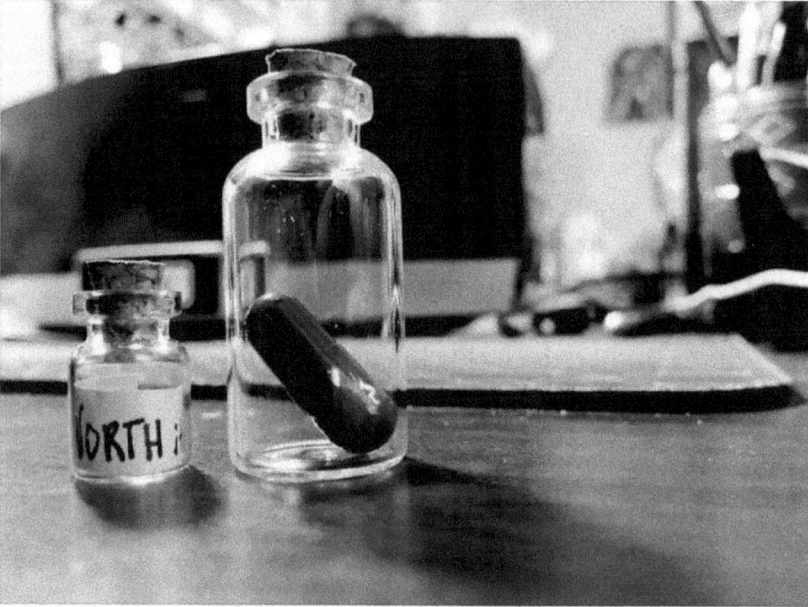

Holly Caudle
2 hrs

My activator pill and my grounding statement🥄🌑😌

👍 Like　　💬 Comment

👤 **Jackie Barros VanCampen** Robbe!!! So many amazing stories with the Xpill! Holy moly! #youareagenius

👤 **Steph Ibbotson** I did an X take. I focused on a feeling and didn't say any words, just took the pill. I was focusing on being happy and after I took the pill I had a series of encounters that were funny with colleagues, got an invite I wasn't expecting to something fun and had a really great, uplifting day. About halfway through the day I got an aha moment - all of this was because the Xpill put me in a position to see the positive and approach everything from a happy place. It was awesome!!!
Like · Reply · 4 mins

4

Jackie Barros VanCampen
11 hrs · 🌐

Such an awesome Sunday! Got house chores done; planned tomorrow's schedule; got ready for my 7-day clean eating/Shakeology challenge; listened to Make It Count by John C. Maxwell; and had an Xpill activation with Robbe Richman which helped me get all the things on my list done! And I even got to spend quality time with the kids! I rate this day a 10!

👍 Like　　　💬 Comment　　　↪ Share

And I've loved reading people's reflections…

"Something magical is happening because I have booked more massage clients than ever. I am happy, energetic, calm and feel well appreciated. I look forward to slowing down a little this weekend to close some open loops and enjoy some quiet down time. This whole Xpill process has been amazing!!!!" – Sarah Fey

"The illusion that it has to be difficult to 'work through our stuff', the illusion that we have to spend years and years in therapy or in meditation before our freedom can be found and lived. I now think it can be instant and as instant as we allow it to be. I think this is one reason Xpill can be so powerful. It provides a conduit for us to make an instant change if we so decide. - Rachelle

The X in Xpill is whatever you want it to be. – Amir

X: The Story of a Magic Pill

You're about to find out what they're talking about…

NOTE: As the reader and co-creator of this experience, you're certainly welcome to read this book in any order you'd like … If you're the type of person to skip all the introductions, go straight to Chapter 2.

Preface

What brought you to this experience?

Did someone inspire you, or was it random?

Either way, it means you're curious, like me. So we already have that value in common.

Whatever the reason, I wonder…

- Do you have a lot of decisions to make?
- Are you feeling overwhelmed?
- Do you know what you want but don't know how to get it?
- Are you frustrated that all the work you're doing isn't going anywhere?
- Is there something big calling you, but you're not even sure what it is?
- Or maybe you do know, but it's quite scary.
- Or you just don't know what to do next and you're looking for clarity.

If you answered yes to any of these, there's a surprising answer that awaits you.

This book is built to help you get to the next level.

I don't know what that is for you. It might be a new job, a relationship, or starting a business. It might mean finally feeling at peace with your life and living in the moment. It might be establishing a new habit, like going to the gym.

Something has already come to mind for you. Maybe you've given up on it. Maybe you think it's just not in the cards for you. Maybe you feel so frustrated with yourself that you haven't gotten it—after all this time, after all these books, after all these programs.

What is gnawing at you? What's the opportunity you're not taking?

Come with Me On a Journey

You're about to read the story of something that has created a major shift in my life and in the lives of others. Shifts like new relationships, careers, starting businesses, getting to the core of deep blocks, discovering true passions, overcoming overwhelm, and breaking through our own resistance.

The way I have done all of this is with a pill; only it's not the pill that did it. It has nothing to do with the pill, and yet everything to do with it. I know it's confusing, but this (and other paradoxes) will make sense if you read on…

What's In Store for You?

In this book I'll share the real, untapped power of the human mind. Feel free to skip to any chapter that seems the most interesting to you.

In each section I will share the:

- Concept
- Stories
- Three powers
- The method I used to create a breakthrough in my life or those of others
- The next steps to use the power in yours.

The Pill

At the center of this experience is a pill called the Xpill, and here you'll learn what it is, how it came about, and why it's so powerful. I'll share:

- My own story and desire to make movies into reality
- How I took the movie *The Matrix* and made it real
- The science behind the pill
- The experiences of the first people to experiment with "The Red Pill,"
- The creation of the Xpill

The Xpill is not a pill; it's an experience… and you'll learn why because I'll share the power of:

- Pills
- Symbols
- Metaphors

What's interesting is it's *not* the pill; you can use all of these things in whatever you're doing!

What creates the context for the experience is the people who are there for it. I'll share with you how people (and what they do) make all the difference.

The People

- The Power of Ritual
- The Power of Witnessing
- The Power of Presence

Any good story has a beginning, middle, and end, with some fascinating drama in between. A great experience is no different. Here I'll explain how you can create it.

The Process

- Introducing the Activation
- What's Key is the Emotion
- The Power of Focus

- The Power of Experiments
- The Power of Small Wins

But first I think it's most important to go into the why...

Introduction

Why this book? Why now?

We have more choices than ever.

Change is happening at such a fast rate that it's hard to deal with.

The amount of uncertainty in our world can leave the strongest of us feeling powerless.

I believe we could use a tool to bring us back.

I notice the same thoughts on repeat—in myself and others—and they sound something like this:

"I have way too many things to do."

"I feel totally overwhelmed."

"So many priorities. Where do I start?"

"It feels like everyone needs something from me."

"My inbox is exploding. I may need to declare email bankruptcy."

"I go into Facebook just to return a message and then I get lost there for half an hour."

"What do I do with all of these notes I'm surrounded by?"

"I have a lot of ideas. Which do I focus on?"

"I get aggravated and irritated without even having a good reason for it."

"I constantly feel tired."

I listen to people talk this way (myself included), and I wonder what they really want. What's at the core of this? One word keeps coming up:

Clarity

I think it's no coincidence that this is something alcoholics desire most; they call it "a moment of clarity." It's that feeling when everything feels clear and understandable. When you know what to do next without question. When the path is laid out in front of you. It's that feeling that you're in the right place with the right people at the right time.

And not just alcoholics crave clarity. We all want it. Even if we are not substance addicts, we are addicted to certain behaviors and thoughts. Let me speak for myself, and perhaps it will resonate with you:

I feel addicted to:

- Staying busy
- Being productive and efficient
- Checking my email

12

- (Trying) to get organized
- Getting on Facebook twenty times a day
- Constantly being on my phone
- Thinking about what I'm going to do next rather than being present
- Thinking I need more _____
- Feeling incomplete
- Feeling like I need to accomplish more before I can have [my soulmate, peace, money, etc.]

Shall I go on?

We're all addicted to something. Twelve-step programs are usually only for diseases that have a tremendous impact on the sufferer's friends and family, but our own personal addictions can keep us from having the life we deserve, and they keep us from connecting through meaningful relationships.

I want you to know this addiction is not your fault. It's happening at a subconscious level. And it's happening due to patterns and conditioning that come from our environment, which can overtake anyone.

This book is for those who want to take their lives back.

And you'll see how you can do it with the power of a pill, people you trust, and a process that opens you up.

Who This Book Is For

Before you read on, consider this:

What if whatever is holding you back from reaching the next level is beyond your awareness?

What if you can't think your way to the next level?

What if decision-making is actually a physical act and not a mental one?

What if you can only create an experience that brings you there?

This book is for…

You the Individual

For all the reasons we've discussed thus far, this can be a platform for breaking through blocks and adding power to new commitments. If you're anything like other Xpill clients, you've probably "tried it all." You've probably done a lot of self-help work, read a lot of books, and taken a lot of programs that have not worked for you. When you read the powers in each section of *this* book, I think you'll see why this approach is different.

You the Coach/Therapist

This is a tool to help with your clients. I get that this is controversial, and it seems almost cult-like to put a pill in front of someone. But at its core, these are pills with no active ingredients.

Wait, what?

Yes, you'll see why when you read the backstory. And in the process section you'll learn how you can use it for laser-fast coaching that empowers clients to make a choice, take action and examine the results (rather than just thinking about it and procrastinating).

You the Educator

Do you have a class, a training, a skill you're teaching, or an experience you are creating for people? The Xpill can enhance any program and help to make it stick, or at least help your students become aware of why they are not completing it.

If you are the coach, therapist, or educator, then we recommend you think about this process first from the lens of the individual (meaning *you*). If you're going to consider it for them, they will want to know that you've done it yourself and approve of the process.

The next few chapters are going to be about the backstory. If you'd rather watch the video, go to Xpill.com and click on the story section. And if you don't care for the story at all, feel free to skip to the main sections.

Who Is This Book *Not* For?

This book is not for you if you're unwilling to get completely real with yourself.

It's not for you if you're unwilling to accept that what holds you back may be beyond your conscious mind.

This book is not for you if you're just looking for the easy way. It may be as simple as a pill, but this process can bring up the resistance, pain, outdated beliefs, and blocks that are holding you back. After all, if you knew what was really holding you back, you'd get through it. Perhaps there's more to your reality than meets the eye. It was this curiosity that lead me to the first discovery…

Part I: The Pill

Chapter 1: Experimentation and Play

The most exciting phrase to hear in science,
the one that heralds new discoveries,
is not "Eureka!" (I found it!), but "That's funny…"
—Isaac Asimov

The scientific method is outstanding because it transcends beliefs. It's not about opinions, viewpoints, or dogma. It's about having a hypothesis, running a test, and learning from results.

This makes it sound like I had some kind of idea of what I was doing. The truth is, I did not…

My Desire to Make Movies Real

I'm most known for my work in company culture. I was the culture strategist at Zappos.com, and I co-developed Zappos Insights, the division that trains companies on great company culture and world-class customer service.

At the same time, I've always done a lot with personal development (life coaching, therapy, Tony Robbins work, and others). I completed Georgetown University's Leadership

18

coaching program, set up the Zappos life-coaching department, and I've coached a lot of people; both personally and in the corporate world.

But my story really begins with a fascination with movies.

Movies have felt like the pinnacle act of creation. You can create *entire worlds* that don't exist.

With our favorite movies, the characters feel like our friends, and we watch them over and over like we're revisiting our favorite vacation spot. I can't tell you how many times I've watched *Star Wars*, *Top Gun* and *The Matrix*.

Movies weren't just my world on the screen; they felt like a natural part of my real world. Growing up in Los Angeles, I was surrounded by the industry. Every kid's parent was an actor, a producer, a director. It all felt so accessible. This was the 1980s, the pre-paparazzi days. You'd see stars all over the place, and no one would even bug them! I remember waiting to board a flight and Tom Hanks was right there next to me.

I wanted to make movies, so when it came time to pick a college I looked for a great film school, in a whole new world outside of LA. The clear pick was Northwestern in Evanston, Illinois. It was top-ten rated, with a big football culture and a famous film and acting school. Perfect. I applied early, got in, and coasted through the rest of high school.

What happened next surprised me.

19

As I watched the film crews working their butts off late into the night for the shortest of scenes, I had a new thought… *I don't want this to be my life.* And even if I did, I didn't have incredible stories that I was dying to get out of my head. In that moment I realized:

I don't want to make movies. I want my life to *be* a movie.

And so that's what I set off to do. Experience many lives and many adventures.

My primary medium was careers: Bartender, waiter, software tester, journalist, marketer, consultant, coach. I ran a fashion company and a magazine. I was a spinning instructor, ran an online community, started a web development company, a co-working space, a crowdfunding site.

And with different jobs came different locations. I've lived in Las Vegas, New York, Boston, Washington, D.C., Chicago, and Austin, Texas.

The larger movie of my life had a running side plot. Tons and tons of self-development. Extensive work in Landmark Education, Tony Robbins, kabbalah, meditation, extended fasting, astral projection, lucid dreaming, and—of course—years and years of therapy. It felt like endless searching. I was always trying to find answers, explanations. I was constantly moving in and out of relationships.

20

They say the grand irony of all self-help work is that you're finally happy when you stop focusing on yourself. Serving a higher cause, devoting yourself to a relationship, creating a world for our children—the deepest, most fulfilling parts of our lives seem to make this notion of "the self" feel quite small.

In this book I'm sharing what has become my higher calling. It connects the world of movies and self-help through the character arc we all experience in our lives: The stories of transformation.

Most exciting for me, this is a story about going from the imaginary to the real, from intangible to tangible, from abstract to reality.

Turning my life into a movie was like the first part of the second act. And then one day, it all shifted. You see, in film school I realized what a big pain in the butt it is to take an idea and turn it into a movie. But what if we reverse the filmmaking process?

What if we took a movie… and made it real?

Chapter 2: First Experiments and Making *The Matrix* Real

"You take the blue pill, the story ends.
You take the red pill, you stay in Wonderland and
I show you how deep the rabbit hole goes."
—Morpheus to Neo, *The Matrix*

This quote is from the famous scene in *The Matrix*, and it follows the classic Joseph Campbell myth structure (we'll discuss that later and how it bridges the world of movies with our own lives).

Neo follows the call to adventure, and he's faced with a choice to cross a threshold. He can take the blue pill and go home, or he can take the red pill and see the truth. The pill is symbolic. He takes it, and does so quite easily. What happens next is a roller coaster as he nearly has a heart attack when he realizes his current world is not real.

Many people use the "red pill" as an analogy for waking up, or crossing a threshold of commitment. But why just make it a metaphor? Why not make it real?

The First Red Pill Experiment

That's what I decided to do. I was heading out to Burning Man; A big, week-long, temporary city in the Nevada desert. Life and art are one—people are all in costume and they're building structures, vehicles, and experiences out of sheer ideas. It's normal to see driving cupcakes, fire-shooting dragons, and even a party on a full scale 747 rolling through the desert.

The whole event runs on a gift economy—no money is exchanged, only gifts. And I wanted my gift to be the Red Pill... I looked for what I could use. It had to be red, and it had to be completely safe.

All I could find were red (cinnamon) Tic Tacs. I ordered new prescription pill bottles, made a label for them, and filled them with the mints. I created instructions that read, "Take this pill and say, 'I want to know my reality.'"

Along with all my other gear, I was carrying eighty vials of pills to Burning Man. I was shaking as I went through TSA security. I wasn't doing anything illegal, but it did not look innocent!

At Burning Man I wore a button on my backpack that read, "I have the red pill." Honestly, I felt afraid to take out the bottles, so I didn't. First I decided I wanted to be of service. My friends had told me that the best experiences happen when you're in service to others, so my first move was to go around asking how I could be of service. I went to different camps and no one would accept my help!

I soon became frustrated and thought, Okay, time to take my own "pill." I opened up a bottle and took one out. I said, "I want to know my reality," and then swallowed it. Unlike Neo, I didn't wake up in a spaceship, but I suddenly had a new thought, a realization about my world. The thought came in someone else's voice, and it said, "You only want to be of service so that people will love you. Just go straight to what you want."

All of a sudden it felt like the facade dropped. I wasn't trying to be of service; I was just being myself, and I felt like I had arrived. I felt more present. I felt noticed. I was having a great time, *and*… I now had a way to be of service. Excited, I headed out to show people the red pill and help them wake up to their own realities.

Cut to three days later, and people were following me through the desert as if I were Moses, waiting for me to get back to camp where I could give them their bottles of pills. People were thrilled, excited, and started having breakthrough thoughts like I had. Even funnier was that there were other people who had a negative reaction when I showed them the bottle.

They said, "I love my reality, man. Get that away from me!" Inside I thought, *Wow—that is a violent reaction to a red Tic Tac!*

I had so much fun giving the bottles away and taking people through the ritual. And I thought I would leave it at that. It's

24

Burning Man, I thought, a whimsical gathering in the desert. Of course people are willing to believe a red Tic Tac can wake you up. It's not actually real. Is it?

And then, I got a phone call …

"Hi, um, I met you at Burning Man, and you took me through the red pill ritual. I was wondering if you have more of the bottles."

"Yes, I do, why?"

"Well, I'm a psychologist, and I decided to do it with my clients, and they're having big breakthroughs that were not possible before this."

Wow.

What blew my mind is that this was not done deceptively. The moment you see the shape and then taste the cinnamon, you know it's a red Tic Tac. And yet her clients were not only willing to try it, but they actually were having breakthroughs.

I realized this wasn't just for fantastical desert playgrounds. This could be real. So I decided to run a bigger experiment, and the results were shocking.

Before I get into that, let's talk about the power of pills.

The Red Pill (Part 2)

I put a question out on Facebook, asking, "If the red pill were real, would you take it?"

The comments came streaming in, and I invited everyone to a private group and shared the idea with them. Only this time, I took it to the next level.

I used a red-colored vitamin. Also, I made it very clear what it was. There was no deception here. People could read the ingredients and research them before taking it.

But this time I had my friend and roommate Holly onboard, and we created an entire experience. We used glass bottles with cork tops, a secret bookcase, and a journal with instructions. The quote on the front was, "At last…" (That's what Morpheus said when he met Neo for the first time in *The Matrix*).

For the first pill we all said the words, "I want to know reality." But the real magic came within the next thirty days. We instructed everyone to commit to something for thirty days.

And even though the commitments were all very different, one by one they were happening. Here are a few quotes from the group:

"Within the context of ritual and a virtual group process, for 30 consecutive days we declared a particular intention, a deep longing or desire around fulfilling our potential. With no turning back. All in.

For me this served to keep my intention squarely in the forefront, and thereby serve as a sort of focusing tool. Like when you make up your mind to buy a particular new car, and you start seeing that model everywhere."

— David Brown

Only later did David realize it went beyond that...

I wasn't connecting the dots between my personal experience and what was happening in my business. I've seen a significant shift in my coaching practice this past month in the number of private referrals I've been getting (and converting) vs. referrals from affiliates. I've been much more forthright about my stand for people living conscious, purposeful lives and that has been reflected in my work (and the growth of my clients). And I've had an odd sense of centeredness and flow... I found myself letting that go and relaxing into that, which is not what I expected but what I needed.

This idea of letting go would later become a big theme in the experience of the Xpill. But I'm getting ahead of myself. Back to the results...

"I moved into a neighborhood that I've always wanted to live in, restarted salsa dancing after an almost six year sabbatical, stopped watching TV, and began reading and really enjoying my spare time. The most notable thing that I've seen shift in the last month is that I've started tapping back into my intuition."

— Holly Caudle

While the instructions were to commit to one intention, it seemed that people got a lot more, and so they didn't just use one, as (another) David found himself shifting his intention the moment he took the pill:

"I'm waking and when it's time to take my red pill, the words come into my head, and sometimes they're [sic] the same as the previous day, sometimes it's a completely different phrase. Whatever the phrase comes out as, it's perfect for that day. Each day gets stronger and stronger. I'm finding distractions fading away much faster. In the past I would sometimes get caught up in distractions for days or even weeks when it would come to breakthroughs that would trigger those subconscious fears. Now, I'm finding the distractions from those triggers lessening as I'm more comfortable making quick decisions and moving on them."

— David Caren

David's story reminded me of Michelangelo removing the pieces of the statue that were not relevant. Like David's experience, it wasn't about will power or driving force. The

29

distractions seemed easy to clear. In other words, what's irrelevant becomes irrelevant.

Like letting go, this _{theme} of clearing out what is unnecessary, outdated, and irrelevant also became themes of the Xpill experience. But to discover that, we had to do more experiments and ask more questions, including:

1) What would the experience be like with a truly inert pill (not just a Tic Tac or a vitamin)?
2) What would it look like to do it live, in-person?
3) What would it look like if it were a group experience?

First, I had to make my own pill ...

Chapter 3: The Xpill, Science, and Powers of the Pill

"Red pill, blue pill. Why not take both?
That's what we'd do in the 60s."
— Ken Wilber, while watching *The Matrix*

I called up a supplement company and told them I wanted to create pills with nothing in them, just an inert substance. They told me I couldn't. They said that's placebo, and it's illegal to market something deceptive. I said, "Actually I'm going to tell them exactly what it is. The ingredients will be right on the bottle." They said they'd never heard of that before … and we manufactured a sample run of 1,500 pills.

When they asked what color, I said purple, for a few reasons:

1. Purple was my favorite color growing up.
2. Purple is the energy chakra connecting to our higher selves.
3. Purple is what happens if you take both "the red pill" and "the blue pill."

The idea is that we can have new experiences and knowledge without leaving our world. In fact, when writer/philosopher Ken Wilber added his commentary to *The Matrix*, he said, "Why not take both pills? That's what we'd do in the 60s."

31

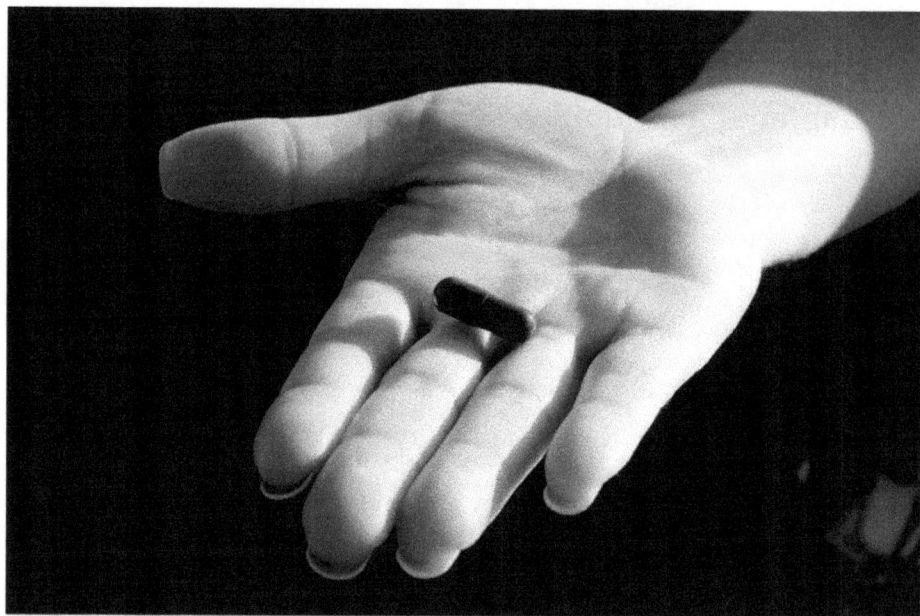

It was clear that this was no longer "the red pill." It was also not the "Purple Pill," which is a well-known trademark for Nexium, and I'm very respectful of that. So what was it, then?

When I presented this quandary to my friend and meditation teacher Scott Schwenk, he said, "Duh! Take the pill to find out its name." Wow, was it really that simple? It certainly made sense.

So I held the pill in my hand, and I said, "By taking this pill, I will know its name." Right after that I sat down and closed my eyes so I could be open to the answers. Many words came into my mind, but one was crystal clear:

Xpill

Xpill made so much sense. The "X" is whatever you want it to be. It's whatever you want it to mean. You create the meaning. And the X factor is the effect, which can be anything.

Buying the Domain Name for Xpill

I was able to find the domain Xpill.com on sale at an auction site, which really felt right. Considering iPill.com is on sale for over $100,000, I wondered how I would ever get the Xpill domain. Long story, short, I was able to get the domain for $12—that felt like a miracle, and definitely a sign that we were on the right track.

Live and In Person

Now that we had the name, the pill and the site, it was time to take it to the next level: Live, in person with people. You'll see that these examples are very goal focused, but what really activates the pill experience is the emotion behind it. There are a few core emotions that we want to feel: joy, flow, peace, clarity, ease, fun. People keep coming back to these words.

Let's get right into it:

ROB: *A new career.* We've found that there are really just two places to start for an Xpill conversation. Either:

a) What's really frustrating you?
or
b) What do you *really* want?

33

The reason is because there's energy there. Our desires and our frustrations have the passion and excitement to drive a real change. So when I sat down with Rob Bakhshai, our conversation went like this:

"What do you really want?"
"I want to have a photography business."
"Great, why do you want that?"

We delved further into both the why and the emotion that the answer would give him. This is key because at the end of the day that's why we're doing anything. There's something we want to feel and experience.

Next comes getting specific.

"What would start this business?"
"Having a website up."

After we get specific then we add a date. Rob got really aggressive.

"I want it by tomorrow."

It could see it was clear in his eyes that he wanted to do it, and he was willing to stay up all night if he had to. So I gave him the Xpill, and he said,

"By taking this Xpill, I will complete my photography site by tomorrow."

He was about to take it when he stopped. We call this last minute resistance. It's when we get hesitant, when resistance comes up, when we doubt ourselves. I asked him what that voice was saying.

"I'm concerned that if I'm up all night, I will be so tired tomorrow that I won't be effective for my students."

So I said, "Okay, let's build that into your formula. Add that you will feel totally energized tomorrow."

He did. He took the pill and felt a surge of energy. He actually sent me a video of him in the car on the way home, singing at the top of his lungs. The next day I got an email from him with the link to his new website. The day after he said he was energized that whole next day, *and* he got two photography clients.

David: Creating His Legacy. Holly and I sat down with David Caren and his wife, Heather Rodriguez. We both knew them as our amazing healers of ZenRoseGarden.com, so it was a pleasure and an honor to now be facilitating a breakthrough for them.

David said he wanted to be rich. When we explored the reason it was to leave a legacy for his children, and the emotion he wanted to feel was powerful. Next, we got specific. What is the very first step in getting richer?

"Creating my next product."

David had a meditation product in mind. And Heather quickly chimed in. "He talks about the product but he doesn't do anything. He seems to have time for video games but not the product."

I think we all can relate, on both sides of this experience.

There's usually a voice that represents the resistance. When I asked David why he didn't work on it, he said he didn't have the right equipment. We got through that quickly (considering anyone with a smart phone can record a high quality audio product).

Having his partner, two witnesses, and a pill right in front of him gave David the space to process this whole picture until he was ready to commit. He said,

"By taking this Xpill I will complete the first draft of my product in two weeks."

And right after he took it, he started to shake and get hot. We were surprised. There's nothing active in the pill, and yet this was a very physical reaction. As a sharp coach he immediately realized this was not a bad thing (even though it was uncomfortable). He was just moving through the resistance.

Two weeks later, David called me and said, "I didn't get it done in two weeks… I got in done in two days!"

The process not only helped David work on his goal, but we heard it helped in his relationship with Heather, who was then inspired to use the Xpill herself.

So as you can see, the Xpill is a tool for commitments and making things happen. That said, it's not just about getting things done, it's about learning along the way.

You might be surprised to know that two weeks after Rob launched his photography business, he shut it down and sold all of his camera gear. Was that a failure or a success?

"For years I had it in my mind that I wanted to be a pro photographer. It wasn't until I actually did it that I realized it's not what I want." Rob continued to use the Xpill everyday and went on to realize his true calling.

These stories were about work, but we've also seen people use it for love. Holly, who I mentioned earlier, is an example of this. Here's her story.

Holly's Story
by Gali Kronenberg

Holly didn't let a day go by without checking for messages left on her dating profiles on Match, Tinder, and Plenty of Fish. A special education teacher in her early thirties, Holly says it wasn't that men didn't ask her out, but that she was meeting "wrong guy after wrong guy." Still more annoying were those times when she felt she had met the "right kind of guy," and they both appeared to have a really nice time together. "It felt devastating to meet a great guy and then never hear back from him."

After seven years of trying to find a relationship, it got to the point where even her dating apps hinted that things were hopeless. "They literally ran out of matches for me." Instead of receiving fresh pics of guys who lived in a fifty-mile radius of Las Vegas, Holly received the message, "Sorry, but we have no one to offer you."

Not ready to give up, Holly signed up for almost every self-help workshop out there. She also voraciously read self-help books about finding the perfect partner and healing her life. It got to the point where she'd leave the library with a stack of eight to ten books on dating, health, and happiness. "I just became this self-help junkie."

Before long, it wasn't just her love life that felt stalled. Even Holly's chosen vocation, working with kids who have severe educational problems—a job that once inspired her—left her exhausted and drained. She used to return home from work and invigorate herself with a run. Now, she found herself returning home from work and collapsing in a heap on the couch. 2014 had been a difficult and lonely year, so when New Year's Eve arrived she wasn't sure she even wanted to go out. Nonetheless, when her friend Robert (Robbe) invited her to a New Year's Eve celebration at his home, she accepted.

The party was intimate. A group of eight friends had gathered at Robbe's for what he described as a ritual to help each of them clarify—and then manifest—his or her highest intention. "Every culture has its own symbols," Robbe explained. "One of the most potent and powerful ones today in our culture is the pill."

Then he told them about his idea to adopt the symbolic power of that symbol to help spur personal breakthroughs. The paradox of Robbe's "Xpill" was that he acknowledged it was a placebo, nothing more than a few grams of rice. Robbe spoke passionately about the scene in the film *The Matrix*, where Morpheus offers Neo a choice between a <u>red pill</u> that will allow him to learn the truth about the Matrix, and a <u>blue pill</u> that will return him to his old life.

As the clocked ticked down to midnight on New Year's Eve, Holly and the other guests each took a turn declaring their intention to the group. Holly felt overwhelmed with resistance. "All my fears came up," she said. "What if I manifest the wrong guy? My mind flashed to my failed marriage."

It took all of her courage to declare aloud to the group that her desire was to manifest "the love of my life." After a few deep breaths, "I looked down at the pill," Holly said, "and swallowed it with a few big gulps of water."

"When you take the Xpill, you cross a threshold," Robbe said. "You could say it's a moment of truth."

Holly had been single for seven years without one solid relationship since her divorce in 2008. Her brow became damp with sweat, and a deep sense of panic welled up inside her. "It felt as if I'd made a vow," said Holly, "and I couldn't take it back."

39

Each guest left the party with a thirty-day supply of Xpills. Everyone agreed they'd take the Xpill daily as a way to reconnect to their intention. Holly placed her bottle on the kitchen counter. Some mornings she restated her exact words about her desire to manifest a life partner. Other days, she'd tweak it and say, "By taking this Xpill I give and receive love freely."

Even spotting the bottle of purple Xpills on the kitchen counter reaffirmed her inner vow. Taking the pill felt far more powerful than merely writing down her goal or repeating an affirmation. "You hold the pill in your hand. You put it in your body," said Holly. "When I read self-help books, the exercises were all about plans for the future. This ritual put my intention in the here and now."

Still, the love of her life didn't show up right away. But everywhere, she said, were signs of change. Suddenly, among the guys who asked her out were a doctor, a pro athlete, and a multimillionaire. "I had moved from a D game to an A game," said Holly. "The guys I was now dating were good men, not jerks.

"I was happy about the change, but I still wasn't convinced a little pill could bring me the love of my life." Still, she had begun to feel a ray of hope. "Every day pushed me to a new level of clarity." She saw signs of change in all aspects of her life. "Sometimes, I just got this strong intuition to do something that in the moment didn't seem to make sense."

One day, Holly felt an impulse to renew her passport. She thought it might be for a potential job overseas, but that proved not to be the case.

The Xpill was beginning to have a positive influence on a lot of areas in Holly's life, not just dating. "I needed a housemate who both loved dogs and would take care of mine when I was away. The first person who responded to my ad was a huge dog lover, loved watching my dogs, and was the perfect housemate."

It had been months since Holly had laced up her Nikes and headed out for a run. So one day, she took the Xpill, saying: "I run effortlessly and with a lot of energy. " And later she reported, "I easily ran six miles, and it felt great!"

When months later she needed to move and find a new place, the first house she looked at was perfect. The problem, she learned, was that sixty other people had also submitted applications to rent the same house. Nonetheless, the following morning, the landlord called Holly to offer it to her.

For Holly, the Xpill was akin to a daily vitamin. "I took it each day as a way to reconnect and recommit to my purpose."

The New Year's Eve guests from Robbe's party called in for periodic phone sessions to discuss how their intentions were unfolding. In one of those calls with Holly, Robbe said something that really hit home for her. "The Xpill provides a focus on relevance and irrelevance."

"That's exactly what was happening to me," said Holly. "In every area of my life, barriers began falling away." Still, Holly lamented to the group, "The Xpill made me fat!" She had set an

intention to diet and eat less. Each day, she'd state her goal
swallow the Xpill. But rather than lose weight, she gained eight
pounds.

Then it struck her. "I don't want to diet. I want to indulge. I
want to eat whatever I want!" She realized that "the Xpill can't fix
a problem I don't want fixed." And she very much wanted to keep
enjoying the food she loved. That's when a deeper and truer desire
surfaced. "My focus became simply to be happy."

Funnily enough, that's when the excess pounds began to fall
away. Instead of fussing over calories and denying herself the
foods she loved, Holly focused on how she wanted to feel. The
happier, safer, and more peaceful she felt, the more the emotional
hunger that drove her to overeat disappeared. Then she felt able to
eat what she loved, enjoy it, and feel satisfied. Food was no longer
a substitute or a source of guilt; it was simply one of life's
pleasures.

It was no coincidence that this was when the love Holly
had been looking for showed up. A few of her college girlfriends
were in town, and her desire was simply to have fun and show her
friends a good time. The women were out in "Old Vegas" on
Fremont Street, near the vintage hotels and old-time casinos
emblazoned with bright lights. "A British guy approached us," said
Holly, who greeted his overture with ambivalence. It was late. And
the British guy and his friends got talking with Holly and her
friends. And then they had a few drinks. Holly paired up with the
British guy, Neil, and without noticing the time pass they fell into

a deep and intimate conversation. Neil put his arm around her, and together they watched the sunrise.

Things with Neil "just felt right." "Just the way he looked at me," said Holly. "I felt cherished."

The catch was that Neil lived in England. They'd met on a Thursday night, and he was due to leave Monday. Had she just met "The One" only to have him disappear? But Neil didn't want things to end either. He rebooked his ticket to leave a day later. After Holly dropped him off at the airport and before Neil's flight departed, he texted, "I want to come back and see you."

Two weeks later, he was back in Vegas.

That's when it became clear to Holly why months earlier she had renewed her lapsed passport. She was now able to accept Neil's invitation to visit him in England. Soon trips to Paris and Barcelona followed.

In a dresser drawer, Holly came across an intention she'd scrawled on a piece of paper a year earlier. "I live a fun, free, and spontaneous lifestyle full of travel with the man I love.

"The velocity of manifesting keeps picking up," said Holly. She married Neil, and the couple have already found their Vegas "dream home." The experience of taking the Xpill enriched her career, health, and prosperity. But Holly says that for her, it will always be "a love potion."

X: The Story of a Magic Pill

❋ ❋ ❋

Can love happen in a moment?

Holly's story evolved over months, but we've found the Xpill can work quite quickly, even in love. Though the result is not always what people expect. In fact, "That's not what I expected," is the phrase we hear most.

Love at the Dating App Party
(This is a great example of what we call an Xpill Activation, which I'll explain later).

I was invited to a party to promote a dating app and asked to speak about Xpill. After sharing the story you've read I invited someone on stage to help them find love. I asked for a volunteer and I went with the first person I saw.

She came up to the stage, and I asked her what she wanted. She said she wanted to be in a relationship. And then I went through the activation process and asked her why she wanted a relationship and what emotion it would give her.

She described her answers, and I asked her what movie scene we would watch if she had that relationship. She began to describe the scene in her living room where her boyfriend was on the computer and she was watching TV.

As she was explaining the scene I noticed her facial expression changed, and she seemed to be getting more tense. I asked what was going on, and she said she felt this tension in her body, her inner chest. I asked her to feel into it and just be. Often this will clear the tension, which I imagine may be some type of fear or memory, but I'm not sure. I just know that when we let ourselves finally feel it that's often the time when we can release it.

This time, however, it wasn't changing. I sensed that this feeling might be blocking another feeling, so I asked her what was behind it. She said "Behind it is this desire to get out and be free." Noticing this was a change in direction, I asked her if she still wanted to use the pill to get a relationship. "I'm really not sure anymore," she said.

I told her there was no pressure to take the pill and she could certainly take what she learned and leave. She was about to do that, but then I asked, "Is there something that you're sure you want?"

She suddenly lit up and said, "Yes! I'm sure I want to feel wild and free!" Then I asked her if she wanted take a pill for that, and she lit up and said *yes*! The whole crowd got excited and yelled. She took the pill by first saying her statement, "By taking this Xpill, I am excited and free," and then she swallowed it. Everyone gave her a round of applause for being so open and vulnerable in front of the crowd.

I noticed that for the whole rest of the party she was totally lit up and excited, feeling like she could really be herself. She was looking forward to a cruise with her best friend. And I had to wonder… in this new emotional space, would she meet somebody she would really want to spend more time with? (Note: Right before publishing this I found out she had an amazing tryst while traveling and is now open to a relationship).

More on Love

Jill used the Xpill to bring love into her life. As we've seen, it's not simply taking the pill. It's the process and people involved as well. Her coach had her write down every non-negotiable. There were 27 including basics like being healthy and generous, to specifics such as liking dogs and being free of addictions… She took an Xpill for each one, and soon after met her man who met the criteria, who (oddly enough) was actually right there in her own apartment complex.

"I had to really get in touch with my emotions, feel the frustrations and clear out space for what I really wanted. It was then that I could get clear on my needs and commit to my own standards."

I also used it for love and it changed my life…

I had an emotional dinner with my friend Melissa. I was really frustrated with dating and I broke down in tears. She looked at me and said, "Why don't you use the Xpill to declare you're ready for the one. So the next morning I did just that. And that day my plane was delayed five different ways, landing me stuck in a city where I met a woman I knew from facebook. We went out for a drink, and rather quickly I found myself in love with her, and began to visit her all the time.

But that's not the interesting part of the story...

What we've found with Xpill is that if you're in alignment, things can happen pretty quickly. But if you're not in alignment, whatever is blocking you will come up. And that relationship became incredibly difficult and tumultuous. I realized all the ways I was not being fully myself, not being open and transparent and authentic. In other words, I realized I actually wasn't ready. They were very hard painful lessons to learn and the breakup left me in a total daze to the point that I couldn't even work. But I realized it's all happened to get me ready.

The Science Behind Placebos

Some say there is no such thing as a placebo effect with the Xpill because there are no effective ingredients. So there is really just a placebo response, which varies from person to person. And most people believe that you have to deceive someone for the placebo to work. Not true.

At Harvard University, Ted Kaptchuk runs the Institute for Placebo Studies. They ran a test using an "ethical placebo," meaning they told people they were getting an inert pill. But they went a step further and informed patients that their research has found placebos can be helpful for their irritable bowel syndrome

(IBS). They found that placebos actually worked when people knew the context, and that people felt more relief. Since then, Kaptchuk has studied the neuroscience of the placebo response, and yet his quote here is very telling:

> "Nobody would believe my research without the neuroscience. ... People ask, 'How does placebo work?' I want to say by rituals and symbols, but they say, 'No, how does it really work?' and I say, 'Oh, you know, dopamine'— and then they feel better."[1]

But it's not just about the patient's belief. It's about the doctor's belief as well, according to Edward Shorter, author of *Bedside Manners*. He has seen how the clinician has to be convinced of the effectiveness to get the placebo effect in the control group.

If you think about it, how much relief do we feel when a doctor says, "You're going to be okay." We immediately feel at ease. And then consider the opposite effect: How would it feel if a doctor tells us their doubts and their worries? When we stress, the stress can cause inflammation in our bodies.[2]

---

[1] http://www.smithsonianmag.com/science-nature/why-i-take-fake-pills-180962765/

[2] https://www.sciencedaily.com/releases/2012/04/120402162546.htm

The Placebo Response Is Part of Real Drugs

The placebo response is so strong that it even works for real drugs. Two groups were given a pain reliever. One was told it would relieve their pain, and the other was told nothing. The group that was told it would relieve their pain found greater relief, even though both pills contained the exact same active ingredient. In Ted Kaptchuk's words, "Morphine given without a person knowing—surreptitiously, in a IV drip—is 50 percent less effective than when it is given in front of them.[3]

Now let me be excessively clear that this book and the Xpill are all about using this work for personal development, not for medical usage. That said, we've also found that the same context applies. It's the entire story, the promises and the expectations of a product or service that are the "active ingredient."

It's beyond placebo…

Jill Richmond experienced the power of the story and expectations. She was struggling with what to do with her career. So we took her through what's called an Xpill Activation (more on that in the Process section or see Xpill.com/activation). It's a ten-minute session in which we dial in the clarity. Jill realized she wanted to be more polarizing—meaning she wants to take action true to herself even when it might upset others.

---

[3] https://www.vox.com/science-and-health/2017/6/1/15711814/open-label-placebo-kaptchuk

Within a day she ended her business partnership of three years. The next day she took another Xpill to commit to sending out a letter to her network. The next day three new opportunities came in. She was on fire, and... she ran out of Xpills. (I had only left her with nine because I didn't have a full bottle with me). She had been taking them everyday with her vitamins, and she wanted to make sure she continued.

"That's okay, I'll just use my fish oil pills," she said.

The next day I got a text from her...

"I am depressed. WTF???"

She was dumbfounded. Unlike all of our other participants who watched movies like *The Secret*, Jill was a very scientific, data-driven person, and to her this made no sense. To her, the fish-oil pill should have worked equally as well.

"Well, let me just ship you a bottle of Xpills, and let's see what happens," I said.

She got them two days later.

"OMG. I feel so much better."

Granted, this is just one story. One day I would love to run a study of Xpill versus an unbranded placebo. My belief is that when there is a bigger story developing, when there is more than just a generic product or experience, then a set of expectations

50

begins to build and we live into those expectations. There is a snowball effect for all who use it.

That's what we are building with the Xpill.

My friend Michael Liskin said it well in his text:

"Dude!

You didn't create a placebo.

You created a play-cebo!

This is about playing with it. Nobody plays with placebos but you. They study it. They avoid it. They hope it isn't so, etc.

You bring them play. That was the missing ingredient."

It's true, our groups and sessions are so much fun.

And with the Xpill you get to choose what it means. There is no dogma. There is nothing you have to believe. There is just experimentation and play.

Once you have the pill right in front of you, the experience has begun because you can't help but wonder what you might take it for. You can take it or not, but once it's there, the fun begins!

With that in mind, let's go over some of the elements that drive this experience. It will not only help you understand what's going on, but it will help you design experiences for yourself and others.

The Power of Pills

We all believe in pills. Think you don't? Keep reading.

What is your relationship to pills? I grew up scared of them. I felt terrorized that I might choke on them, and it took a long time for me to even learn how to swallow them.

It couldn't have been just me because years later my high school girlfriend sat across from me at the Cheesecake Factory, facing her antibiotic pill and those same fears from childhood. I coached her to put it as far back in her mouth as she could and take a gigantic swig of water.

In college, I very reluctantly went on antidepressants. I didn't want to admit that I wanted help. I wanted to believe it's all within me. But after a few weeks on them I felt fantastic. They say antidepressants have the strongest placebo effects because the condition of depression is hopelessness. Thus, anything that gives you hope can be the cure for you. I noticed this when a friend of mine took an antidepressant and said he felt better the moment he swallowed it. It was far too fast to be a physical reaction from the substance of the pill.

I felt so great on the antidepressants that I did not heed the doctor's warnings. They said I should stay on them for at least two years, so that I could change my lifestyle and habits. But because I was feeling so good, I believed that I had changed for good, and I went off them within three months. Of course, I felt depressed again a few months later. The pills certainly had a huge power over me, and I would have been much better if I had followed my doctor's advice and stayed on them. Regardless of whether it was the placebo response or a real chemical change in my body, the pills were very effective.

We have all had an experience in which a pill did something to alter us. Whether it was for a headache, an infection, or just trying to get high, we have all had an experience in which a pill changed our state.

Even if we don't take pills, we believe in their power. In other words, if I gave you a cyanide pill, would you tell me you don't believe in its power and just take it? No way.

So what does this mean for pills with no active ingredients in them?

The Power of Symbols

A pill is a modern-day archetype. An archetype is a symbol that is universally known; however, the meaning becomes different to each person. Jung showed us how the subconscious uses symbols in dreams to speak to us.

For example, you might have a dream about a bear. The meaning of that bear would be different to you and me because we have different emotions in the dream. For me it might mean I'm not being aggressive enough at the office. For you it might mean you're not being protective of your family. Different meanings, and yet the qualities of a bear remain consistent. This is the medium of the archetype.

Modern-day archetypes have made their way into the collective conscious. For example, consider a phone or an airplane. If you believe (as I do) that dreams are speaking to us through symbols, it begs the question:

What if we could speak back to our unconscious mind with symbols?

If we could do that, then we could start to reprogram ourselves.

What if that symbol could send a command or start a search query for information like a search engine. If we could communicate back to our unconscious mind, then it would help if we could speak its language. The unconscious doesn't speak English. It speaks in symbols.

The pill is a symbol of transformation or change. Think about it. You feel a certain way—stomachache, headache, nervous, sad—and you take a pill to feel something different. Or people take them recreationally to achieve a high state or a relaxed state. So the Xpill is all about sending thoughts and feelings via the symbol of a pill.

This pill is a symbol of commitment because once you swallow it you can't go back. It's in you. You are already in a new state of mind like Holly and I were that New Year's Eve. So it's one thing to say "I will write a book by the end of the year." It's another thing to say that and take a pill with it. And the experience becomes even more powerful when you have witnesses (We'll cover that in the People section).

What amazes me is how much power the pill has as a symbol, even if you don't swallow it. Something powerful happens when you simply use it as a conversation starter. You place a pill in front of someone and ask, "If you could take this for anything, what would you take it for?"

I know people who carry the Xpill around with them just as a prompt to think about what they really want. It truly begs the question about, and gets us to focus on, what's important rather than getting lost in day-to-day life.

The Power of Metaphor

It seems that everything comes down to meaning. We want meaningful work, a meaningful relationship, a meaningful life. We're often inspired by books, movies, and songs. So how do we actually create meaning? And how do we actively share it?

X: The Story of a Magic Pill

"The meaning of meaning is metaphor."
—Marshall McLuhan

Metaphors are how we take the abstract and make it real.

They're how we communicate about something so far out there that we can't truly understand it without using metaphor.

Take money. We all get it, but you might not realize how. The way we communicate about money is completely based on metaphor: The metaphor of water. Notice how every phrase connected to money is based on water:

- Cash flow
- Pool of assets
- Revenue stream
- Rainmakers
- Liquidate funds
- Trickle down economics

And take computers. They are far too abstract for us all to understand. It's all code. That's why computers only went mainstream when Steve Jobs and Steve Wozniak took the XEROX interface of a desktop (metaphor) and built it into the computer we know today.

Computers don't need the metaphors, but we use them to understand files, folders, trash cans, and mail much easier than we can understand code.

Think of marriage. What's the metaphor? It's a bind, a ring on your finger. In reality it's just a piece of metal and a rock. But there is so much meaning, both for society and for those two individuals. We give it the meaning it has.

The Xpill is nothing but a capsule with inert powder inside. It's nothing. But the power of a pill has so much meaning to our society.

My Story: Finding My House

We've noticed that when we use the Xpill for general clarity, we don't tend to get an answer. But if we get very specific then there's a greater chance of it working. Since I was able to use the Xpill to trigger my intuition to discover the name, I decided to use it to help me find my house.

I was about to sign a contract for a home in L.A. It was a fantastic place. Brand new, great structure, every element I was looking for... although I really did not like the area. Still, I had been looking for so long, and I really wanted it. And yet, I had that doubt. So I took the Xpill with the intention of learning if this was the house for me.

I held the pill and said, "By taking this Xpill, I know the right home for me." And then I swallowed it.

I sat still and closed my eyes.

I started to see two vague images. I could hardly make them out. One was of a house close to the beach. The other was a blue umbrella. And I was upset that this was the message because there was no way I could afford a house by the beach in L.A. No way. And yet, it did at least give me the confidence to turn down the deal.

I still had no idea what to do. In fact, I went and lived in Austin for six months because I'd always wanted to.

And then I went on a trip to San Diego. I loved it there. My family vacationed there when I was growing up, and I had fond memories of the beaches. It was like a chilled-out version of LA. I walked around the beach area and found a gorgeous $3 million home (ridiculously out of my price range).

The realtor was there and said, "Come on, make an offer, you never know." I said, "Okay, $800,000." He sarcastically said, "Let me get your name so I can spell it right on the contract!" We laughed, and he asked me what I was looking for. I described my criteria, and the next day we headed out in his car.

We visited several places that I thought were terribly expensive and not that great. As we were driving, I looked around the Redfin app, and my eyes lit up when I found a gorgeous house, in my price range, near the beach, with a pool. *No way*, I thought.

It must have been off the radar for people who were looking for a single family home because it was listed as a condominium.

My mouth nearly dropped when I saw there was a blue umbrella in the backyard.

How to Use the Power of Pills

1. Try them out for yourself at <u>Xpill.com</u>
There are several options to engage, starting with:
Level 1 — The Activation: You can get the Xpill in kit form to take on your own.

2. Try using your own pills or mints.
Personally I don't find this as effective, but some people do. You can use all of the techniques with your own pills (more in the Process section).

3. Take any supplement or pill you're currently taking.
- Ask yourself why you're taking it.
- Start tracking how it actually affects you.
- Get clear on the power it has (or does not have).

Part II: The People

Chapter 4: The Group Experience

"Two or more people actively engaged in the pursuit of a
definite purpose with a positive mental attitude, constitute an
unbeatable force."
-Napoleon Hill, on the Mastermind Principle

So far we had done a lot of individual work with the Xpill through
one-on-one sessions or by people taking it at home. Next I wanted
to try it out as a group experience, live and in person, where
people would take it at the event.

The Transformation Leadership Council

The Transformation Leadership Council is a group formed by
Jack Canfield, co-author of the Chicken Soup for the Soul series.
It's the legendary tribal council from the movie *The Secret,* with
members such as John Grey, Marianne Williamson, Lisa Nichols,
and many more.

I had the honor of joining as one of the youngest members after
they saw the transformational work I've done for company culture.
My first meeting was both exciting and intimidating because I felt
like the weakest link. At my second meeting, I led everyone in

improv comedy exercises, and by my fourth I was ready to present the Xpill.

I gave a TED-style talk about how I came up with the concept and why I believe it works so well, and then I did a live activation on stage. Before the activation we did a Q&A session. Everyone was laughing so hard by the time the talk was done because it's such a ridiculous idea... and yet, it's really working for people.

The first comment was, "So no one really knows what's inside the pill when you give it to them, right?" I said, "No, everyone knows. I have never deceived anyone." I had somehow left that out of the presentation.

When I asked for a volunteer, I went to the first hand that shot up. Arjuna Ardagh answered the call. If you don't know of him, he created Awakening Coaching—a technique so powerful that the first time I experienced it I felt myself entering a vortex like the experience Eckhart Tolle describes in the prologue of *The Power of Now*.

Arjuna is a bald man, and he asked if he could use it to get his hair back. The crowd laughed, and I said, "That's a very off-label use that is untested." He was joking, but he was very serious about his real intention.

"I want to have no to-do list."

The crowd was instantly skeptical, and when I opened the discussion up to them, they directly challenged him.

"Maybe you just want a *better* to-do list."

"No, I want no to-do list."

"Maybe you want a better *relationship* with your to-do list."

"No, I want no to-do list."

It is very powerful when someone is crystal clear about what they want. That clarity can trigger others, or draw others to challenge us to check if we are truly clear.

Mike Rayburn, author of *What If*, assumed this role. "Arjuna, are you sure you want this? If you were accused of a crime and sent to jail you would suddenly have no to-do list. Be careful what you wish for."

Arjuna felt like everyone was trying to get him to take the blue pill! Finally Katherine Woodward Thomas (author of *Calling in the One*) stepped in and said, "Let's allow Arjuna to have his process. This is his decision." And at that, Arjuna said, "By taking this Xpill I will have no to-do list within three months."

He said he felt good.

Then I got everyone into triads to pick one person to do the same process with them (I go over this process in the Activation section of the book).

Waves of energy and laughter traveled across the room as people coached each other before finally taking the pill. After the session I asked for people to share about their experiences. We had run over on time, so we only had time for one share.

Mike Rayburn's wife stood up and said she had asked to feel the love of God through her husband. And through tears she said she had butterflies in her stomach and that she hadn't felt this much love since they'd first met.

Jack Canfield later came up to me and said he felt so great that it was like he was euphoric. I asked him what had happened.

"Arjuna's intention inspired me to clean my desk. But when I said that to my group, they asked why. I said because then I can get more work done. Again they asked why. I told them it was to write more books, and with each why we got closer and closer to the truth, which is that I just want to feel loved. So I took it for that and instantly felt euphoric." Two days later I asked him how he felt. He said the feeling had not stopped (You can see his video at Xpill.com).

The morning after the experience, Arjuna came up to me and said, "It's done! My to-do list is gone!"

What?! He'd said three months. It had been less than a day.

"I had a new thought after taking the pill."

This is common from what we've seen. After people make the commitment, the unconscious mind seems to go to work to provide us with the solution.

65

"I called up my assistant and said, 'I'm going to give you my full to-do list. You do everything you can, and what you can't do, I want you to schedule as an appointment for me in my calendar, but only for that day. No others. That way I only have a schedule to follow and no big back log that I see."

His assistant's reaction was priceless. "I have been waiting a long time for you to say this," she said.

We've found many uses for the Xpill. Our daily use section will show you more. For now we've covered two:

1. Committing to doing something (create a website or a new product, make a change)
2. Feeling something (love of God, being loved)

And it's worth knowing about the third:

3. A result, outside of our control

We call this the Wildcard Experience because you just don't know what you're going to get. Perhaps nothing.

Jennifer took the Xpill saying, "I will make a billion dollars with my business." One could say the exact opposite happened. Her business fell apart very quickly after this (within a week). When she told me, I thought she would be very upset and curse the pill and the process. Instead she had the opposite response. She said it was only through this experience that she realized she didn't want to be in that business and didn't even want to be a CEO. She changed her business entirely, and she's much happier now.

So it seems that our deeper intention may really come to the forefront.

This theme of the "opposite" seems to happen at various times when people take the Xpill...

I remember when I had a big task to get done: I had a proposal due, and I wasn't even sure what to propose. I felt like it would take all day. My normal course of action would be to push through and drink coffee. But this time I took an Xpill to commit to writing it, and I was surprised to find myself immediately tired. I've learned *not* to assume that "this must not be working" and simply go with the flow, so I went with it, and I took a nap. I woke up so refreshed and my mental clarity was so present that the proposal was clear to me; I wrote it and sent it within an hour.

A task I thought would take all day only took an hour, after I had a physical reaction and then went with it instead of trying to fight it.

The group Xpill experiences after the Tribal Leadership Council got even wilder. We've seen all kinds of reactions, from euphoria and high to anxious and nauseous. A lot can come up when we cross that threshold and take the desire from an outside thought to literally putting it inside our bodies.

Is there a potential that the pill causes something physical through its substance? Only if you believe you can get a reaction from the inert ingredients that are listed on the side of the bottle. Otherwise it's our minds at work.

Even when people have a "negative" reaction, they know it's their own psychology. That said, I realized we have a responsibility to create very safe experiences with trusted guides. That's why I've included very specific instructions later in this book for using the Xpill, or any other pill, with intention. (And I want to mention again, this is not meant to diagnose or treat any kind of medical or psychological illness.)

What amazed me at the next group experience was how the pill works… when people don't even take it… what?

It Can Work for Those Who Don't Take It

I was in the islands of Greece, at one of the most awesome group experiences outside of Burning Man. Vishen Lahkiani, CEO of MindValley, invited me to speak at Afest, an incredible event of world-class speakers held at beautiful locations around the world. Vishen had seen me speak at the Transformational Leadership Council where we are both members. He wanted me to hand out the pill to everyone at Afest like I had done there.

The night before going on stage I got the feeling that simply handing out the pill to everyone, especially those who are not trained coaches, would not be the best move. I told Vishen that since people have all kinds of reactions to such a powerful ritual, I only wanted to do a few demos on stage.

I delivered the speech (you can watch it at Xpill.com), and two things happened. The first, which was that everyone asked me for the pill, was not so surprising. The second was how many people came up to me and said they'd had a breakthrough just hearing the stories. They saw what's possible, and seeing possibility gave them the clarity to make new decisions.

One man came up to me at the party afterward and said, "Since I saw you speak I've decided to get a new job, change my city, and leave my relationship." I thought he was completely making fun of me and being facetious.

I said, "Ha ha," sarcastically and with disdain in my voice. "I get it. You think I'm ridiculous and all of this is crap, right?"

"No," he said, "I'm dead serious."

I had to ask him several times to repeat himself because I was so incredulous.

"Call me in six months," he said. "You'll see I'm serious."

I did. And he had done everything he said he would.

Other people have reactions that are not a positive take on the speech, but still impactful.

One gentleman left while I was speaking because he thought it was all baloney. He came back later, and when I asked people to share their thoughts, he raised his hand.

"I left to the bathroom and said to myself, 'Those people are idiots in that room. That pill will never work.'… The instant I said that, I thought about my wife. Everyone in my life believes my relationship with her can work, while I'm the only one saying it will never work. Then suddenly I realized … everyone in the room was having a grand time while I was alone in my misery in the bathroom." Tears came down his face as he said, "In that moment I realized my wife is the most beautiful, wonderful person I know."

It's powerful when you realize that nothing is stopping you but your own mind.

Teams and Masterminds

It was twilight time and I was in Hawaii, standing on a railing that overlooked a volcano. The group in front of me was the Mavericks, a high-end mastermind of entrepreneurs lead by Yanik Silver (founder of the Underground Marketing Conference). I delivered the speech and handed out pills with the instructions on our activation process. People used the pills throughout the weekend as a tool for their larger commitments.

Yanik then used the pills with his own team…

"I used the Xpill with our internal team as the final step in setting our yearly planning. There were tears, hugging and deep, deep alignment...unlike anything we've ever done together. And again we locked it in with the Xpill. There is significant power is in the intention, ritual and physical artifact of the process. It's awesome!"

- Yanik Silver, founder Maverick1000 and author Evolved Enterprise

Lisa Sassevich is an incredibly successful coach. She is the best-kept secret for many speakers because of her sales tactics, which are authentic instead of manipulative. She had me speak to her mastermind group, and after I spoke she said,

"Every year I run a number of high-end, two to three day retreats for clients who have paid 20 to 100K for the complete year-long experience. So I have to always find an amazing experience for that level of client, something that makes a deep and lasting impact in their lives, and all I have to say is thank you, Robert! My clients are still thanking me for the experience we had, and we had renewals on site because the experience was so magnificent. It was safe; it was respectful. People were inspired to step up and grow big."

Xpill for Groups and Masterminds

See the video at Xpill.com/events

Chapter 5: The Power of Ritual, Witnessing, and Attention

"This is what rituals are for.
We do spiritual ceremonies to create a safe resting place
for our most complicated feelings of joy or trauma,
so that we don't have to haul those feelings around with us forever,
weighing us down.
And I do believe that if your culture or tradition doesn't have the
specific ritual you are craving,
then you are absolutely permitted to make up a ceremony of your
own devising."
—Elizabeth Gilbert

There is a magnificent power in partnership, in teams, and groups. What brings us together is a purpose. But what keeps us together are our habits—a family spending a weekend together, a sports team practicing together.

What if we create our own habits?

The Power of Ritual

Rituals are the habits of a people. They are passed on from generation to generation. They serve as rites of passage: getting

73

married, having Thanksgiving dinner or Christmas celebrations. Ritual is the staff meeting or the quarterly review.

I've noticed rituals are extremely powerful in the corporate realm. The companies that commit to daily scrums, weekly stand-up meetings, and quarterly reviews and celebrations tend to be the most successful. Zappos still has the company "take a day" quarterly for a big review and party, and Google still does weekly town hall meetings with the founders. Rituals are group habits.

The same way making a habit of going to the gym can help you meet your fitness goal, our social/cultural rituals consistently help us meet our emotional and spiritual goals. Ritual slows us down, brings attention to detail, and acts as a counterbalance to our addictive thoughts and behaviors.

Xpill is designed to be a ritual, complete with the classic and simple structure that includes:

- Both universal and individual meetings
- A beginning, middle, and end
- A "master of ceremonies" who facilitates

And it actually begins before it begins. People look at the Xpill questions to gain clarity on what they want (see examples at Xpill.com/decider). Often people will walk around with the pill, hold it and contemplate it, or talk about it with others.

(NOTE: A more detailed version of this can be found in the next section on process.)

They get set up with their pill and their water. They log in to a group video call. They clear all distractions, and the activator asks about what it is they want. Or sometimes the activator asks what it is they want to let go. (Note: Xpill can be taken by yourself, with a partner, with a trained activator, or with a group. See Xpill.com/groups).

In the middle, they collaborate to get clear on the intention, the feeling, and the wording, which is the statement.

And finally the end is taking the pill. Or not. Remember, it's all invitation. It's all opt-in. Sometimes people get to the end of the process and find they're not ready, or that they've discovered a whole new piece of information through the activation process. Just coming to the table and facing a decision point is enough to create new learning. Most of the time people really want to take the pill.

And just as there is a beginning before the beginning, there is an end after the end. People often notice a new thought, a new feeling, an insight, or have a new choice to make later that day.

It's all activated because they took an abstract desire and made it specific.

The Power of Witnessing

"Can I get a witness?"
—Dr. Dre

Of course, that quote is actually Dr. Dre quoting many ministers, who all know the power of having people present for any kind of declaration.

In the most basic terms, if I am in a room all by myself and I declare that I am writing this book by the end of the year, then there's a certain level of charge. But that level is dramatically increased if I livestream my intention on Facebook to my thousands of friends. Suddenly it's very, very real.

Having more people present is a driver in the sense that I feel more accountable, but having just a few people in an intimate group is emotionally powerful. With Xpill Activations we like to have a few people present because they offer the support, questions, and curiosity to help someone get clear on their intentions and then help them create their own statement for the pill (the words that ride on top of the emotion and the intention).

A positive side effect is the way the witnesses are moved by the person in the activation. I've seen people moved to tears by the emotion, or sometimes they are inspired by it. When we do small group activations in the morning via video conference, people will often "piggy back," meaning they hear someone's statement and decide to make it a part of their own. Often people will come to the calls unsure of what to do, and the group will inspire them and help them get clarity.

Groups that have consistent activities have a certain formula to them, a ritual. Whether it's the ladies getting together for a game of Mahjong or an Alcoholics Anonymous meetings, there is a certain protocol, language, and beginning/middle/end that holds it all together for that particular activity and makes it repeatable. This is the Power of Witnessing.

The Power of Attention

People want to be seen, heard, and validated.

The fast coaching approach to the activation with witnesses places a lot of attention on a person. The attention people receive when I have them on stage is so strong that they can be moved to tears. But all it takes is one person with focus. No distractions, no cell phones. And as you'll see in the Activation section ("The Process"), direct eye contact is key.

But for now, let's just talk about what attention can do.

I remember when I was at Zappos and a reporter from *Harvard Business Review* came through and said, "I have visited so many companies, I've met with the heads of state, and I have never felt as warm and welcomed as I do here." A tear came down his face as he said, "I want to bring my family here to experience this."

I asked what "this" was. I was thinking he would say there was some big profound conversation, but he said, "Honestly, it's in the little things. It's even the way people look me in the eye, smile, and say 'Hi, how are you?' I can really feel it."

Exquisite attention makes a difference, both inside the company for its employees and outside for the brand. It is such a scarce resource that when we truly give someone our whole attention, it's a gift like no other.

Stewart Emery is the co-author of *Do You Matter? How Great Design Will Make People Love Your Company*. He's the man who led the meeting at MasterCard when they figured out the iconic campaign "Priceless. For everything else, there's Mastercard."

When he was advising a coffee company, he asked,

"What business do you think you're in?"
"Coffee."
"Everyone is in that business. You're going to lose playing that game. You're actually in the business of making people's day."

He said they needed to remember people's names, to connect with them, remember their likes and dislikes, that sort of thing. But the way to do so was not with hospitality training. It was with attention training. He had them practice the coffee-making techniques so many times that they could do it without even looking. That way they could maintain eye contact and keep attention on their customer.

That is how they kept growing the brand.

My Story: Running the Las Vegas Marathon

The only time I ever got close to running a marathon was jumping into the last six miles of the Marine Corps marathon to support my friend Raj. Even though we walked some of the time, I was sore for a week and my knees would buckle just going up stairs. A few years later I would need knee surgery, and they've hurt on and off ever since.

I lived in Vegas for five years, and the marathon looked like so much fun. You could run down the Strip at night to music. When I went back years later I saw that the marathon was happening the next day. I called Holly, my Xpill co-founder, and asked if she wanted to do it. We both had no training, and it was the next day. We decided to do the half-marathon, which was only thirteen miles. Still, it was twice as long as I had ever run, and I'd had injuries the last time I'd tried.

"Let's test what the Xpill can do," I said to Holly. We had seen our friend Lee take it and shave 29 minutes off his triathlon time, so we said, "Why not?" I realized that as a leader I want to go first in testing something that I considered "not possible."

We took it together and shot video of the whole thing (You can see it at Xpill.com). We set the intention to run the whole thing while having fun and in perfect form. (I was going to say with no injuries, but we've learned that including negatives in the intention does not work).

With no training at all, we ran the whole thing. I had no soreness, and my knees were completely fine.

I mention this story because the "people power" was having thousands of screaming fans and an army of runners to be with. I have a feeling that if I had run the same distance by myself on a road it may not have worked. That's the power of a great group experience.

How to Use the Power of People

There's a power to group activity. It's why exercise phenomena like Crossfit have taken off. Even the kind that people participate in at home, like P90X, are filled with videos of other people so that it at least *feels* like you're in a group. Here's how to use the Power of People to maximize your Xpill experience:

1. Throw a party

You can order several Xpill activation kits, have people watch the backstory video (either together or before they get there), and then have fun working with each other to zero in on your intentions.

2. Join a group

Our Xpill experience took a quantum leap forward when we created groups to meet online. A group can be incredibly powerful, with or without a pill, if you are all there to support each other. In our Xpill programs we help you form the group and give you guidelines on staying focused and creating amazing experiences for each other.

3. Create a yearly ritual

The first time we took Xpill outside of Burning Man was for New Year's Eve. Having people together and setting a big intention for the new year can be very powerful.

Part III: The Process

Chapter 6: The Activation

"A powerful listener can shape the entire conversation,
without even saying anything."
—Dave Logan, author of *Tribal Leadership*

What's so powerful about the Xpill is that it's process-oriented —
meaning the steps themselves reveal what's at the core (as opposed
to needing a certain skill). In fact, in our groups we often say,
"Stop trying to figure it out." Figuring things out means looking
for rational reasons, and that can be a wild-goose chase when the
real answer might not make sense. You'll see what I mean when
we get into our process.

The process we use is called the Activation.

The word *activation* is so perfect, because to me it implies
something is already there. Something is dormant. It's within you,
just waiting to be turned on.

We call it that because there is a moment in the conversation
when it feels alive. Since there's nothing in the pill to begin with,
we say it becomes "activated" when we hit that emotion + clarity.
Of course it's really *you* who is being activated.

NOTE: This can happen at any point in the process. Be on the lookout.

You can do this by yourself, but we recommend activation with other people or a partner. It can be so much more powerful for reasons you'll see. Once you get the hang of how it works you can do it more on your own (though we keep coming back to doing it with others).

The Role of the Activator

Whether it is Obi Wan Kenobi in *Star Wars* or the officiator at a wedding, there is (oddly) a third party who gives us the power and choice we already have within us. In my corporate life I've seen how powerful it is to have meetings facilitated by a third party so the leaders can focus.

The activator is a powerful listener. They are the facilitator and the witness (though there can be as many witnesses as you'd like).

Same for the Xpill. We call the process of aligning your intention and emotion the way to "activate" the pill. And that is done by an activator. Anyone can be an activator, but the most important ability of an activator is powerful listening. Even if you've never had an Xpill, there are probably people in your life (maybe you) who help others with these qualities as well as the techniques in the chapters that follow.

There are ways to know if you have a powerful listener in the room. If that listener is engaged, everyone is engaged ... but if the listener starts checking his or her phone, everyone else will as well.

NOTE: If you're interested in activator training you can go to: www.Xpill.com/mastery

The best activators have been through the Xpill experience themselves. They know the powers we've covered, and they are well versed in the principles you'll read about later. Here's a brief overview of their tools:

- **Exquisite attention.** The activator is very present with participants. Maintains eye contact the whole time and encourages them to keep eye contact as well.
- **Questions and curiosity.** This is the participant's session, not ours. Questions help them find the answers for themselves. When we find our own answer we feel more ownership for the realizations and are thus more committed.
- **Mirroring, not judging.** We can reflect what we see, hear, and feel without projecting our own emotions or desires on them.
- **Empathy.** We all want to feel seen, heard, and understood. It's amazing what we can let go of when we feel deeply understood. Even though the questions can be confronting, there's a gentleness to the process.
- **Abstract to specific.** The facilitator keeps them present by holding eye contact and asking questions such as, "What

movie scene do you want to create?" A movie scene makes us think in real, practical terms that we can all envision.

Remember most of all: it's all experimentation and play! And part of the game (like any good sport) is that there is a limit of time to play the game.

Getting Clear

Most people think clarity is information—a plan, a direction. That may be the form, but if you think about it, clarity is a feeling. Who knows what the "right" or "best" thing is for you. Clarity isn't information. It's a feeling. It's about feeling clear.

After years of experimenting with the Xpill process, we have found that what's most important is the feeling. People do not allow themselves to feel—sometimes it's out of shame, guilt, or fear. Sometimes they are stuck in a bad habit because there's a feeling they do not want to experience. Whatever the case may be, our feelings give us information. And usually, a feeling is what we are all seeking.

I've noticed this as an overall trend of people using the Xpill. We start off with a desire to simply feel good, but what holds us back is our unwillingness to feel what we're really feeling. We do things to get away from feeling it (food, TV, drugs, social media, etc.). But by not allowing ourselves to feel it we develop tension in our body, and then we do things to avoid feeling the tension, so it's a vicious cycle. And it can be stopped simply by facing our reality, acknowledging the truth, and letting ourselves feel it. Doing this is especially helpful one-on-one or in a group, as you'll see.

That's why the first question I ask is simply, "How are you feeling? And we do not judge it or label it. It's simply a feeling — excited, nervous, shaky, happy, sad. We then let the person breathe into it and experience it. Often this level of permission is enough for a breakthrough. When the emotion is fully felt, then we can more easily let it go.

If there is no strong emotion, you can go straight to Step 1.

If there is strong emotion, here is the process I use (what I say):

1. What are you feeling?
2. Breathe into that. Don't try to change it. Just be with it.
3. Let me know if anything changes, and if not, that's fine.

Usually within minutes the emotion will shift, or turn into heat, and the person calms down. If not, they can breathe with it longer, or I ask them to ask their body what it wants them to know (I know it sounds weird, but it works).

You don't have to know what it is ...

People have found tears come and have no idea why. If they come with an insight, it's great, but we've found it's not really necessary to figure it out. You are allowed to simply feel it and let it come over you. Think of it like you're throwing up—yes, it would be good to know why it happened, but even if you can't figure it out, you will feel so much better and clearer by the end of it. As we've found, this process happens beyond a level that's logical. You don't even have to believe in it. All it takes is willingness and openness.

Regardless of what happens here, you can move on to Step 1.

Step 1: What Do You Want?

The process begins for people when they find out about the pill. What's amazing is how much we've seen it affect people before they even take it. Jason Dorsey said, "I keep carrying it with me and thinking about what I'm going to take it for." Once that pill is in front of you, it almost begs the question, like a genie in a bottle:

What is it you really want?

What is the desire or frustration? Where is your edge? Where are you experiencing fear, frustration, excitement, joy, or resistance?

Clarity comes through the entire process, but holding the question is part of the process. We've found questions to be the greatest gift because they inspire new thinking while allowing people to think for themselves. Here are some examples:

- What do I want?
- What would a quantum leap look like?
- What does it look like to me to have a full, rich life?
- What am I obsessing about?
- What am I tolerating?
- What am I avoiding?
- When do I feel my most real self?
- What causes me to feel excitement?
- What would I gain if I let go of this?
- What advice would I give to someone else in my exact situation?
- In what way am I playing small?
- What am I resisting?
- What is the fear? How does it feel? And how can I push through it?
- What will free me up?
- What can I give myself permission to do, feel, or experience?
- What decision have I been avoiding?
- What do I want to do and haven't?
- When was the last time I felt lit up?
- What's next?

Notice the emotion that comes up. That is where the power is. If it's clear, then fantastic. If not, it's usually one of two things:

Resistance

There are many forms of resistance. Often it's something you really want, but you're holding yourself back from it, either by denying yourself, or simply letting other things get in the way. For example if you really want to write a book – What is stopping you?

One question to find the source of resistance is to ask, "What is it about your reality that you're not accepting?" When I asked this of Michelle, she said, "That I'm alone." (She had just broken up with her on and off again boyfriend. It was super charged when she took an Xpill for this. She was terrified.

After she took it she felt a sigh of relief. There's a weight that comes off when we stop resisting and accept our reality.

"Resisting the resistance is like a Chinese finger trap," said Karolyn McKinley, psychologist and Xpill user.

"Resistance is the highest form of progress... The frustration we experience is actually energy building. The overwhelm builds up and it teaches you how to let go that you couldn't do when the energy was at a lower level."
Vivek Mandan CEO of Source

Frustration

You really don't want something, but you're making yourself do it, or feel that you should or have to.

Examples:

I want to tell my speaking bureaus that I am now charging a higher rate, but I've been delaying this to-do item. I know I want this so I expand my income, and also turning down lower-priced gigs will give me more time. That's resistance.

Frustration is thinking I really should do it, but I don't want to. I remember a time when I felt like I should be dating more, but I really didn't want to. I just wanted to focus on my work, relax and spend time with friends. That was more my frustration at thinking I had to be dating.

Three Guiding Forces

There are many guides to dividing up your life. For example, the wheel of life covers topics like finances, the body, emotions, relationships, and spirituality. These models can certainly work to help you determine what you want to use the Xpill for (or for any intentional program). I have found that at its most basic, it all comes down to three areas:

1. Power
2. People
3. Purpose

- **Power**

  Power is all about your own personal power—meaning
  energy, or whatever it takes for you to be okay on your own.
  That includes everything from taking care of your body to
  finances, and anything else that you do to feel like you have
  energy to use in the world.

- **People**

  This means the relationships that are most important to you.
  Those can be your spouse, kids, parents, friends.
  Relationships are a key driver of our happiness (unless
  you're one of those people who live in Alaska by yourself
  with animals, and if that's your idea of bliss, then you can
  just skip this one).

- **Purpose**

  This is how you serve in the world, or what you create.
  What is your legacy? What is it that you love you to do, who
  do you love to serve? What are you bringing forth into the
  world?

  You can pick from any of these areas.

Step 2: Why Do You Want It?

This is key.

What will this give you?

Keep asking why. See if you can get to the core emotion you're looking for.

If you remember, this is what Jack Canfield did.

"I want a clean desk." Why?

"So I can do better research." Why?

"So I can write more books." Why?

"So I can help more people." Why?

"So that I can make an impact." Why?

"So that I can feel loved."

Step 3: Choose Your Activation

We've generally found there are three types of activations. NOTE: There are more uses beyond these. See Xpill Daily Use section.

1. **Commitment** (Rob's photography website)
    This is a crossing of the chasm. It's the commitment to jump, to do that thing, to take that next step. Sometimes the step is clear, like for Rob creating his photography website. Sometimes the activation process brings the clarity, or the next step comes soon afterward (for example, Arjuna and his to-do list plan).

Key question to get clear:

What is the very next movie scene of your life we would see if this happened?

2. Feeling (Jack Canfield and feeling loved)
Any activation includes the feeling, but for this type it's the primary motivation. Often it starts with a commitment (the way Jack wanted to clean his desk), and then it gets to a core emotion. There can be a lot of release in this.

Key question to get clear:
What do I want to be experiencing right now?

3. Result (Jennifer's story about wanting a billion dollars in her business)
This is like a wild card. You are focusing on something outside of your control. We have found with this one that the exact opposite can happen if it's not in alignment with what you really want. Remember Holly's story? She set the intention to lose the weight, but she gained more. She realized her real intention was to feel free to do what she wants, and when she took that on in her life, she found it easy to eat well and lose weight.

Key question to get clear:
What will having that thing do for you?

There are more uses we'll cover in the Daily Use section.

Step 4: Formulate Your Statement

Now we get to the wording. This is the combination of the intention and the emotion. State it in the form of:

"By taking this Xpill, I…"

For example:
"By taking this Xpill, I write for an hour today."
"By taking this Xpill, I am at peace."
"By taking this Xpill, I start my new business."

NOTE: Above all, the emotion comes first. That's what's going into the pill. So for example, when people use the Xpill to get their to-do list done, it usually backfires and they have a terribly unproductive day. We believe that it is because the emotion going into such a statement is based on the fear of what it means to not get it all done.

And all kinds of words can come after that. Usually the first attempt feels very jumbled and incoherent. That's very natural, and it's why having a facilitator and witnesses are very helpful. They help you dial it in.

Let's start with what we've found does *not* work so well, and then get to what does. (That said, remember that this is your experience. You are free to do whatever you please).

What doesn't work so well:

1. Negative statements

Negative statements such as "I don't want to feel tired anymore," or "I don't want to feel like I'm lacking" keep us focused on the lack. The intention and energy will follow your focus, and when it's on what you don't want, then that is exactly what you'll get. State what you *do* want, and find the place within you or the part of your life where you currently have it. Remember, it's the feeling we're uploading.

2. Qualifying words

Words like just, maybe, want, like, can if, and such are qualifiers. For example:

- "I just want to feel good." **vs.** "I feel good."
- "I want to feel like I'm worth it." vs. "I am worth it."
- "Maybe I'll write a book" vs. "I will write my book by December."
- "I think that I'm just going to…" vs. "I will…"
- "I can have it all." vs. "I have it all."
- "I intend to write a book" vs. "I *will* write a book."

Even the phrase "I will" can be tricky. If it's something you are going to do, the phrase is fantastic because it signifies commitment. But if it's used because of a perceived lack, then there's an opportunity to upgrade it. For example, when I was struggling at an event and was worried I had wasted my money, I said, "I will make this valuable." But sensing the forced nature of the feeling, my coach interceded. (Remember, the *feeling* drives everything). And she said, "What if you just said, "This is valuable." I instantly felt better. It felt more like a deep knowing that the value was there and I just had to see it rather than search for it or force it.

If you feel anything after making your statement (peace, heat, nervousness, excitement, fear), that's a great sign that you nailed it.

Other qualifying words come out as disclaimers. They often end with the word *but*:

- "I know it's way out in the future, but…" (and why not now?)
- "I'm sure it's unrealistic, but…"

Another sign is shrugging, which often indicates an inability to hold the sensation. Or it could be that you don't believe yourself, and the body is showing your "tell," like a bluff in poker. Or it could be a case in which the goal is not in alignment with what you really want. If you are the activator, then mirroring that back to the other person with questions and curiosity will help them to reframe their statement.

3. The word "need"

Dave Asprey of Bulletproof Coffee brought to my attention that the word "need" is disempowering. He said that when people use the word "need," it's almost always a lie. Unless it has to do with getting enough air and water to your body, "need" does not literally apply to most situations. So when we are using it, we are lying to ourselves and others.

When Joe Tatta (author of *Heal Your Pain Now*) had his activation, he started with, "By taking this Xpill, I will write this book and give people what they need." His body was tight when he said it, and his voice was tense. This type of statement a) assumes he knows more about what people need than what they know for themselves, and b) people must accept his work for him to feel fulfilled. Putting our own sense of fulfillment into the hands of others is disempowering.

Joe shifted his statement to, "By taking this Xpill, I will complete this book and give people hope." The other witnesses and I felt warm chills up and down our bodies as he said it. It felt great, and he felt far more relaxed saying it. His new statement sounded more like he was offering a gift, and respecting his readers' choice to take it or not. He didn't need them to take it for him to feel happy.

The most basic questions you can ask yourself to get to the core are:

"Is this coming from fear or love?"

"Does this feel light or heavy?"

"Am I feeling pressured to get this right, rather than playing with it?"

What Works!

1. Start with letting go

Letting go means getting out of a story and going straight to what you want. An example of a story is, "I always mess up when I try something new." If that's your story then it's likely to continue. A story is how we project a future based on past experiences, when truth in the future is unknown. It's all just resistance. There are so many excuses tied into why we can't do something. Say it, and then release it. You're clearing up space for what you do want.

2. Dial in the feeling

Feeling what you want to be feeling when you set the intention for the pill is absolutely key. For example, if you use the Xpill to get something done and you're feeling really tense about it, then that's what you're putting into the pill. And if you instead focus on how great you'll feel when it's done and what that will give you, we've found that ends up creating a much more productive and enjoyable experience. Ideally your activator and witnesses help with this. If you consciously or unconsciously do not feel what you want to feel, then I'll explain what can happen in the next section, called "What Happens Right After."

3. Active and present wording

Words like these get us into that space:

- I am…
- I know…
- I trust…
- I believe…
- I claim…
- I let go of…

- I learn…
- I love…
- I forgive…
- I understand…
- I allow…
- I clear…
- I recognize…
- I realize…

Is This Just About Intention Setting?

Some people hear about Xpill and say it's all about intentions. It is… if that works for you. I've found the word can get overused, and in some cases it has a negative connotation (an example is the saying, "The road to hell is paved with good intentions"). I like words such as *statements* and *declarations* because they feel more powerful.

Catherine joined our calls for the first time, and she wanted to create her vision. She said the words, "I intend to create my vision." Again, it's all about the feeling, and it just felt lacking. I said, "How about you say, I *will* create my vision." She replied, "Yes!"

That's the activation we're looking for. Everyone can feel it. Catherine took the pill and screamed right afterward.

I followed up a couple days later…

Today

Robbe Richman   11:22am
Hi Catherine, how is the writing out of your vision going?

Catherine Navarro   11:29am
Omg!!! Amazing! I actually had a writer friend offer to write it out with me!!!
I'm working with a multi-dimensional healer, and I was hesitating writing out my contract with God, as to how I am willing to serve. It felt so scary- so I wrote out a vision as to how I would like to show up. Finished that yesterday.
Today writing out the how I think that will actually look- yay! So exciting! When she offered I almost cried! She offered on Monday- the same day that I activated!

🔲 Sent from Messenger

Attachment to the Words

It's common for people to stress over the wording of their statements, but that attachment is usually just fear of getting it wrong, or that we won't get exactly what we want. Sometimes people throw everything in there, and I say, "Imagine five people trying to get through a door at once. They'll never get through. But if they go one at a time, they'll all get through." Same approach for our desires.

Sometimes different words will come to mind right as you are saying your statement. One time I said, "I am aligned." And yet in my head, I thought, "I am maligned." I paused to unpack it and realized how much I worried that people won't accept me if I am authentic. I got clear on that resistance, let myself feel it, and then went forward.

100

Some of the words and phrases that contribute to lack of clarity are:

- Maybe
- Should
- Reasonable
- Like
- Just
- I think
- I might

Remember, It's All Experimentation and Play

If you have good people around you whom you trust, they'll help you notice if your intention or wording sounds off. And whenever we've heard of that happening, it has just meant more learning.

I've heard people going to extremes in their imaginations—for example, if you wish for free food, you could end up in jail with a lot of free food (NOTE: No one has ended up in jail…yet). But here's the main thing to keep in mind: If you get really in touch with the why and the emotion you want to feel, then you'll likely have a positive experience. You won't always get exactly what you want, but you'll usually have an experience of learning more about yourself, and (according to massively successful entrepreneur Gary Vaynerchuk), self-awareness is the greatest skill we can have.

Step 5: Face the Resistance

Resistance might not come up at all. And if so, that's great!

That said, a lot of resistance can come up through the Xpill process. And that's not a bad thing. I was reminded of this in a Soul Cycle class. The instructor kept saying, "Add more resistance!" It hit me that we were gladly paying thirty dollars to add resistance into our lives! But we like it! It makes it fun, challenging and makes us stronger.

I was in a martial arts class hosted by Jesse Elder. First he had us punch a bag. Next was the same exercise except two people did whatever they could to push and pull us away from the bag. Which do you think was more fun? The second one was way more fun! I had a blast when they laid on the resistance. Put it this way: have you ever heard of a soccer player complaining because there's a goalie standing in the way of the ball? No way. No goalie, and there's no game.

Just the right amount of resistance is both fun and makes us stronger.

How Your Resistance Surfaces

So where do we find the resistance? Ahh, there are many ways:

Ambivalence. We can easily be paralyzed by choice. Ever find yourself feeling torn between two choices? You want to have it all. You fear missing out. Sometimes there's a third choice you're not seeing. Or you can have them both, you just have to focus on one first. I often hear that people want freedom, so I immediately ask, "Freedom from something or to do something?" And it catches them off guard. Most people think freedom in itself is enough. What they don't realize is how freedom without a directive can be completely debilitating because of so many choices. (Some call this a first-world problem).

Frustration. Think about what frustration is. It's knowing there is the possibility of having more, being better, gaining a more ideal outcome, and the difference between that and our current reality. Simply knowing something could be better and seeing that it's not the reality causes frustration. The most visionary people, like Steve Jobs, are constantly frustrated. That's what happens when you have high standards. He made it into a lifestyle, and he changed our lives as a result. How can you turn your frustration into action, or let go of something that's not serving you?

Irritation. The feeling of irritation is telling you to look at something. Perhaps you're irritated by someone else because they remind you of something in yourself. It could be a sign that you're out of alignment, or that there's an opportunity to lean into it. I remember talking to a woman who wanted to be a speaker. Until she said that, I was not irritated at all. But once she told me her goal I found her voice so nasally that I could barely stand it. At first I thought I was being sensitive, but then I realized that it was an opportunity to step into the awkward zone and tell her my observation, because it could have an effect on her realizing her dream. I finally did, and she was very grateful.

103

Lack. Sometimes the voice of resistance will tell you that you don't have enough time, money, or energy to do something. Not only is it rarely true, but also some of the biggest innovations have come out of a restriction of resources. Did you know that's how reality TV started? One story has it that MTV wanted to do a soap opera, but they did not have the budget. So a producer said, "I guess we'll just have to use real people instead of actors we can't afford." And thus a huge innovation in television came from a lack.

Confusion. Another form of resistance is confusion. Why? It keeps us where we are. We are convinced that we don't have enough information to make a decision, so we become paralyzed as a result. But confusion at its core is a feeling, and the act of commitment makes confusion disappear. Speaker/writer Terri Trespicio says, "Confusion is like creating your own traffic jam so that you don't have to actually go anywhere."

Overwhelm. Overwhelm is an inability to hold sensation. We are often overwhelmed by what we ourselves create. Knowing that doesn't make it any easier when our circuits are overloaded. Think about it this way: in electronics the resistor on the circuit gets hot when current is passing through it. You may experience overwhelm literally as heat. I remember my resistance in intimacy: I would get so hot lying still next to a woman that I would have to get up and leave. Or so I told myself. One time I finally decided to stay, even if I felt so hot that I thought I was going to die. I did get really hot and thought I was going to lose consciousness. But something happened. It was like my mind or soul realized I was committed to breaking through, and in a moment the heat disappeared and I felt incredibly peaceful and light.

Anger and Sadness Are Not Resistance

Anger and sadness are actually great signs. They mean you're really processing the emotions. You're letting yourself feel them. Sometimes people will come to tears in the middle of an activation when they feel so seen, heard, and safe. Anger often starts when people think it's about something outside of themselves.

In Silver Wain's activation she said, "I want to write this book so I can liberate all the women who have been suffering." Reading her tone I said, "Why are you so angry about this?" She was shocked. She didn't know she was angry. She thought it was just her passion, but she tapped into that anger and transformed it once she could see it clearly.

Last-inute esistance

After we do all the clearing work within the activation, the resistance may come back right before taking the pill. It can come in the form of excessive wordiness, trembling, even dropping the pill. Some have said it felt like the pill jumped out of their mouth as they tried to put it in (Remember, there's nothing in the pill, so it's most likely the unconscious mind doing this with your hands — ever accidentally dialed someone and found it was not so "accidental"?). Other forms include dropped calls and losing cell phone reception.

So what do we do in this situation?

If the person was clear before this, we encourage them to get really present, centered, and do it again. That often works, but that said, it is *always* their choice. They can adjust it, change it, or flat out not take the pill.

In that Soul Cycle class it hit me that the right amount of resistance is key. You really want to have just the right amount. Too little and it's not a challenge, but too much and you can't keep up with the rhythm of the songs. I've had to learn my own personal levels. Once I even got off the bike entirely because I was feeling sick. I decided to take a rest rather than push it.

Karolyn McKinley said, "I feel like the Xpill helps me dissolve my defenses."

What's also true about resistance is that the more we resist, the stronger it gets. So if we can take it on when it comes up we have less pain to deal with overall. It's like reverse interest. The more you wait, the more you lose.

The game of resistance is all about choosing when to push through and when to surrender and let go.

Step 6: Take the Pill

If the emotion is strong, clear and your words resonate, then it's down the hatch!

If we are in a group, sometimes the facilitator will ask the others to weigh in by either giving the thumbs up (if they feel it's clear), or a level hand to show it's not quite there yet.

That said, remember: it's your pill. Even if you don't have approval from others, if you feel clear and committed then go for it.

1. Get centered.
Don't rush it. Feel the words. Say them slowly. If resistance comes up in the form of dropping the pill or some other way, begin again.

2. Take the pill.
Drink it down with plenty of water. (We recommend taking your pill with a lot of water. It keeps you present in the moment, and most of us could use more water!)

Notice how it feels. Did it go down easy or was it hard to swallow. What did it taste like? You'd be surprised how different this can be depending on the take.

3. Let yourself sit and feel it.
There's tendency to rush or go to the next person, but let yourself take a minute to feel it. Sometimes new thoughts and feelings arise in that very moment if you give them a chance.

Step 7: Integrate

On the other side of swallowing the pill can be all kinds of emotions. We've seen euphoria, excitement, shaking, nausea, peace—you name it. The good news is that when the emotion is "negative," it's been short-lasting and/or it just points to a fear that can be faced.

We've found that many things can come about after taking the Xpill. You may have a new idea, an insight, or find yourself suddenly sleepy. Whether you feel something or not, we highly recommend getting into your body and out of your head... that means going for a walk or a bike ride, taking a shower or a bath. Anything where you are feeling—but without a screen or even a notebook in front of you. This space allows your brain to free associate and make connections that may not be logical but still could make a lot of sense.

Throughout the day, look to see where you can make a new choice. By taking the pill you are opening yourself up to new information, and your unconscious mind is now scanning for it.

Recognize your surroundings. Ask yourself:
- What comes up?
- What song do you hear next?
- Who walks by?
- Who's the first person you talk to?
- What are you called to do?
- What do you feel like starting?
- What do you feel like letting go of?

108

Notice what may even be missing.

The "Opposite" Effect

Sometimes the exact opposite of what you intended can happen. And that's actually not a bad thing—like when Jennifer's business crashed, and she realized she hated the business and actually wanted out. The process actually sped up this other process, and she got to what she loves much sooner.

This can happen when:

- The intention is a wish. When it's something outside of our control, we might have an experience that's out of our control (which can be fun! Or it can be a rude awakening).
- People say they want something but don't have the feeling. That's when we tend to see the opposite happen (or nothing at all).

For example, let's say someone wants to have a smooth, peaceful day, but they are feeling stressed out as they take the pill. Usually the "opposite" happens for them. I use that word in quotes because what actually happens is that whatever is blocking them comes up to be cleared (It's often something they have been procrastinating doing).

For example, this person may get a reminder from her accountant that her tax payment is late. This would be perfectly normal because it could be the tax payment that was causing her stress, and now she has to face it to clear it.

A classic one is taking the Xpill to get your to-do list done. It never happens because the emotion is often the fear of not getting it done, and so that's what's created because that is the emotional focus. Make sense?

We've only covered the first day so far! When people take the Xpill everyday, it keeps going. We'll cover that in the section on going deeper. For now let's talk about one final step and then the three powers that make the activation work.

Step 7: Follow-Up

If you did the activation for someone else, then one of the most powerful things you can do is follow up. I remember how powerful it was with my friend Silvia.

We were meeting for dinner. The sushi was served, and we were about to eat when Silvia started tearing up. We had done an Xpill Activation in New York a couple months before, and now we were both in L.A.

"I just want to thank you for what you did. I was in a really low place." She said the activation really helped, and I asked why. She said, "You could see my light, and I just couldn't at the time. I trusted that your perception was more accurate than mine. And then afterward you kept checking in on me. That really meant a lot."

I learned the power of follow-up in a business context. I remember when I had my first role as a manager and I was hiring. A lot of people who submitted resumes were not a fit, so I sent them an email letting them know. I was shocked to receive an appreciative response that read:

"Thank you so much for writing back. I've been sending out so many resumes, it feels like no one is even out there. Thank you for taking the time to contact me."

Then at Zappos I noticed how knowing about the customer allowed us to create a really strong connection. It's funny because

111

the design of our backend interface looked like it was from the mid-90s, and yet it was so easy to use and had one key feature — the notes stream. You could see all the customer notes in one place, with everything from order detail to personal notes like, "She likes to be called Barb." People felt known and heard because (thanks to our system) we remembered.

Follow-up is giving people two of our most precious resources; our attention plus our memory. In the Xpill process we ask, "Can I follow up with you tomorrow to see how it went?"

People really appreciate when you check in on them, when you ask, when you care. It seems so obvious, and yet we all get so distracted that we don't always remember to do it.

So remember to ask,
"How did your day go?"
"What came up?"
"Any aha moments?"

Share to Keep

I learned a valuable lesson when I was culture strategist at Zappos. People would ask, "How can you have thousands of people tour through your company and still get work done? It must be so distracting to your purpose." Actually, I noticed the opposite was true. Giving tours was a way to share the culture, and by sharing it two things happened:

1. It spread the word about our culture and brand.
2. It helped us appreciate how amazing we had it.

By seeing people come in wide-eyed and so appreciative, we in turn had a constant reminder of how lucky we were.

That's when I learned this paradoxical principle:

What we share we get to keep; what we hoard disappears.

So for this reason I encourage people to share what they learned as publicly as possible—the wins as well as the vulnerability. It inspires others and reinforces the lesson.

I would never force anyone to share, or recommend that anyone force himself or herself to share. But what I have noticed is that when I have the desire to share and I don't do it, I seem to get sick. I've noticed that with others through any self-development process. If something comes through us that we want to express but instead we push down out of fear, it goes toxic in our bodies.

Now, I'm no doctor, so this may be a ridiculous point. But I have seen research that shows stress causes inflammation, and inflammation causes disease, so there may be something to this.

For myself, I've noticed that expression keeps me in the flow while simultaneously keeping me grounded.

And here's a pro tip…

Whatever comes up after your experience, whatever you're resisting, that's the opportunity for the next step and for tomorrow's Xpill.

Chapter 7: The Power of Focus

What's underneath this process, this ritual, is three key factors: Focus, Experience, and Small Wins. You can use their power in your life, even without the Xpill.

John Grey may be the foremost expert on relationships. He's the author of *Men Are from Mars, Women Are from Venus*. Since writing that book he has continued to explore what makes relationships work. He noticed how much diet has an effect on our mood and thus our relationships, so he then wrote about that.

Grey has most recently discovered that the power of focus can make or break not only relationships, but everything else in our lives. His book, *Staying Focused in a Hyper World* is book one in a series of three.

When I consult for businesses, I find that their enemy is not their competitors; it's distractions. There are so many shiny objects, so many goals to chase, so many technologies to try out. And that doesn't even speak to all of the inside distractions for their employees, especially social media (Facebook, Instagram, and others).

115

Paraphrasing David Packard (of Hewlett Packard fame): "Most companies don't die of starvation. Most companies die of indigestion, from trying to swallow too much."

What the Xpill does is focus people on a single statement, a single choice for that day. And the process also takes them from an abstract thought — "I want to be happy" — to a specific action or commitment that will make them happy.

My Example:

"I'm so frustrated! I have so much to do, I'm feeling totally overwhelmed, and I don't know where to start." This was me talking to Holly on the phone. We've learned that the power of questions and curiosity is so much stronger than giving each other advice.

After letting me vent for a while so I could let it all go, she asked,

"What do you want to feel?"

"Peaceful and productive."

"What would give you the most peace and focus right now?"

"I want to focus on the book. I will limit all of my other tasks to one hour or so and then write the book."

Since that conversation, these words have been flowing out of me.

This is highly representative of the Xpill process. It starts off in a jumble or mess of words. It starts with competing desires and commitments. It starts abstract and unclear. Then we get our focus down to one thing, one emotion, or one task.

The Power of Experience

What baffles a lot of people is that the Xpill can have a response when people know there is nothing in the pill. Their typical reaction is that it works because people believe it will work. This assumes that the experience is predicated by the belief, rather than the <u>belief created through the experience</u>.

Let me explain. David Gonzalez was holding the Xpill and said, "By taking this Xpill, I will devote an hour a day to business development." Right before he took it, he stopped and looked me in the eye.

"As your friend, I have to tell you — I don't believe this will work."

I think he expected me to stop him or tell him he shouldn't do it. Instead I replied, "Great. I've never heard anyone say that yet, and I'm up for an experiment if you are."

He took the pill, swallowed it, and we were both caught off guard by what came next. Tears rolled down his face. In shock, he said slowly, "What's happening to me?"

"I don't know," I said honestly. "But something is happening." (Later I would realize this is part of the clearing process—clearing out the emotions that are keeping us from what we want).

And in the end, he did not spend that hour a day, but there was certainly a new emotional discovery in the process. And if I knew what I do now about small wins, I would have recommended that he do that hour for just a few days so that he could have a win with a beginning, middle, and end.

Experiences shape our beliefs. The most challenging way to change our beliefs is by talking (to others or to ourselves), and yet the world of marketing and influence seem to focus more on words and advertising than on creating transformative experiences.

Zappos Insights

Zappos became known as a "service company that happens to sell shoes." And I quickly realized that what I was there to develop—Zappos Insights—is a "belief-changing company that happens to sell corporate training."

My original mission was to create a video site with a monthly membership fee. We hosted an event at Zappos inviting people to learn about the culture, and we videotaped the whole experience. We asked, "How did you like the content?" People said it was "so-

so, but… the experience of being here blew our minds." I asked why.

"We already knew a lot of the content you taught us. But honestly, we didn't believe it was possible for ourselves until we came here and experienced it."

It blew my mind that it wasn't the content—it wasn't the parties we took them to. It was them simply being part of the culture. It was an experience that changed their beliefs.

I could go into more belief-changing experiences at Zappos and other corporate cultures, but that's the subject of my book, *The Culture Blueprint*.

Whether we're talking about corporations, relationships, or your own kids, experiences shape our beliefs. And to have a new experience, you don't have to believe—you just have to be willing.

The Power of Small Wins

"The Xpill isn't just a greater commitment to goals
but a perpetual reminder of micro-decisions
that all lead me closer to my bigger goals."
—Jill Richmond

Marisa Murgatroyd noticed a peculiar anomaly in the world of information products (online courses, videos, trainings, and similar products). An abysmally low percentage of people actually start

119

and finish an information product. Like books that are never read, people pay anywhere from $27 to $3000 for products they never use. And the industry seems to be okay with this. But not Marisa.

She noticed that most of these products overwhelm us with information and tasks, and then we feel like losers because we haven't done them. In other words, we get high from the promise of new skills and a new life, and it all goes downhill from there.

Marisa noticed that what we all want in life is great experiences. And experiences get better and better if we limit information and give people the chance for small wins. So she designed her own product with very short videos and very quick tasks that people can accomplish week by week. People were not overwhelmed, and her program achieved a remarkable 97 percent completion rate.

That's the power of micro-commitments, and Xpill can be used in the same way.

After an activation, the user has a chance to use the Xpill for many purposes (see the section on daily use). We show them how to use micro-commitments every day to build towards the larger goal. Sometimes people achieve their goal so quickly that they'll take a second or third Xpill that day for the next win.

Everyone loves winning, and by breaking the commitments down to smaller ones every day, we build that muscle. And we get those little dopamine hits that keep us going. It becomes an overall great experience, and that's what is key to changing beliefs.

I used the Xpill for micro-commitments to write this book. First I said, "By taking the Xpill I will write at least five pages." I wrote exactly five pages. Noticing that I had stopped at five, I changed the next day's statement to, "By taking this Xpill I will write *more* than five pages." I'm in the middle of that day right now, and I lost count at twenty pages. I'm still going.

These daily wins are huge. We all want something big and massive, but it's way easier to get there one win at a time.

Here Is the Process in a Nutshell

- Ask yourself, "What do I want?"
- Yes, but what do you *really* want?
- Commit to it.
- Clear space and remove the irrelevant.
- Take an action.
- Get support.
- Build the skill.
- Move toward that big goal. The one that scares you.
- Be public about your process.
- Share the learning, and allow others to celebrate you.
- Help someone else.

And here are example statements that people have used:

Goals

Today, I will complete _____ with grace, ease, and flow.

I just do it.

I am ready.

I get out of my own way.

I spend one hour today working on my vision.

I exercise twenty minutes a day for the next four days.

I choose healthy food options for the next three days.

Clearing Space

I release the things in the way of my health.

I clear space for things that no longer serve me.

I let go and have faith that things will provide.

I will put down on paper all things that I've committed to do.

I have a blast processing notes and getting organized.

I release the story.

Mindsets

I live in the fullest expression of my talents.

I commit to knowing that I am enough.

I expand my impact on the world and play big.

I accept that everything is happening for my growth, healing, and success.

I write my own story.

I am complete.

I matter.

I completely forgive myself.

I trust the process.

I love my choices.

Chapter 8: How to Use the Power of the Xpill

"That's not what I expected."
-Many people after taking the Xpill

There are many different ways you can use the Xpill.

1. Try it with a kit or with one of our Xpill Activators.
You can use the do-it-yourself kit, or upgrade to work with a trained activator. www.Xpill.com.

2. Laser coach your clients
The same process can be done with or without the pill. Remember to limit your time to twelve minutes, keep eye contact the whole time, and use the feelings in the body for guidance.

3. Break down your goals into a series of micro commitments.
Any big project is a series of small decisions. Break the big project down and then take it one step at a time.

Xpill Daily Uses

The Xpill can be many things to many people. Some see it as giving themselves permission to do what they really want by externalizing what they crave inside. Others see it as a truth-discovering device, and others as a commitment tool. Whatever it is, it's taken very consciously because everyone knows it's an inert pill.

Also, repetition breaks habits. So whether you're creating a new habit (we like to call created habits "rituals"), or you want to simply live with conscious intention everyday, here are some uses you can play with:

1. Commitment takes
Xpill works for either big declarations, like "I will complete this book by June," or for micro-commitments, like "I will write one page today."

Keep in mind that the emotion overrides everything. For example, when people say, "By taking the Xpill, I will get my to-do list done," they never get it done! Why? Because they are really experiencing an emotion of fear and lack. You'll have much better success if you address one important item.

2. Feeling takes
Through the activations we often find that people are doing something just to attain a feeling. Here's an example:
I want to put up a new website. Why? So I can get clients. Why? So I can have money. Why? So I can relax and finally be at

peace... ahh, with that realization/activation, we say, "By taking this Xpill, I am at peace."

3. Grounding statements

The activation process can bring up a lot of emotions. Sometimes people feel all over the map, and that's when we recommend a grounding statement. It's the one that anchors you to the thought/emotion that keeps you feeling good. Examples include:

- I am safe.
- I am enough.
- I am complete.
- I am worth it.

4. Expansion statements

This is the opposite of grounding statements. Expansion statements are used when we are feeling low and want more emotion, more freedom, more growth. Statements include:

- I am playful.
- I am fun.
- I am free.

5. Clearing takes

Many people are inspired to clear out things that are no longer useful (feelings, things, tasks, even relationships). Statements include:

- I let go of the need to be right.
- I release the old story I have about success.
- I let go of these unnecessary objects.
- I release this on-again, off-again relationship.

6. Acceptance Takes

We've found it's very helpful to use the Xpill to accept your current state, whether you consider that positive or negative. Sometimes people take the Xpill with the statement, "I am frustrated" and they feel more relaxed because they are accepting it rather than fighting it.

Interestingly, the same holds true when it's something positive. Sometimes people are very happy and that can feel "too good to be true," or we can look for the struggle or the problems. Taking the Xpill for acceptance of something positive, such as "I am grateful for my relationship" can help us let go of resisting what we really want.

7. Support takes

Sometimes we take Xpill in support of others. I admit this is very weird… though not so much if you believe in the power of prayer. At times I have found it seems to help another person, or at the very least I feel good about myself when I take it. Oddly, I have gotten a lot done on my to-do list on the days I do support takes for other people.

Xpill Themes

We have found there are general themes that come up. First, it starts with a frustration or desire. The frustrations are usually about money, and the desire is usually for love. While the goals themselves have a lot of range, the underlying desire tends to be one of the following:

Freedom. For some the desire starts with wanting more money, but it's really about freedom. Sometimes it's freedom from something, sometimes it's freedom to do something. The access to this freedom comes by either getting very specific and putting the plan into action, or it comes down to generating the feeling of freedom in the now rather than a future date. In the first case, the action creates the feeling; in the latter, the feeling creates the action.

Higher purpose, true calling. Many people feel they aren't yet doing what they were really born to do. People feel stuck in their day-to-day lives, whether we're talking about a job or just habits. Once again it comes down to feelings and action. The activation helps us get clear on what that calling looks like, and how we can feel the emotion we seek rather than using our higher cause to try to get a feeling.

Love and self-love. People use the Xpill for love—to find it, to keep it, and also for ending relationships and cutting ties from past loves, or just noticing how hard it is to love someone without first loving yourself.

Sub-themes include:

- Dropping stories that no longer serve us.
- Getting into integrity.
- Releasing judgments (which seem to make people tired).
- Clearing open loops (incomplete commitments).
- Finding what's really blocking us.
- A desire to feel seen and heard.
- Noticing our avoidance/resistance.
- Giving ourselves permission.
- Accepting (even loving) our reality, and noticing the peace that comes with it.

The End (or Rather, the Beginning)

Follow the String

Have you noticed that in a movie you never see the characters working on a to-do list for hours? Not only is it boring cinema, it's also not the path of success. Success is a series of steps. Some wins, some losses, a lot of learning. It's a progression, and a new story emerging.

And all that's required of the hero is two things:

The desire and the willingness

It's been a key lesson for me on this adventure because I can easily get overwhelmed and stressed. My tendency is to retreat — to be alone and try to solve it all in my head. And yet, what's worked is just following the string. It's been one speech invitation to the next. It's a contact, it's a mastermind group that will help me. It's all evolving like the Hero's Journey. I just have to be willing, and follow the string.

In *The Matrix*, Neo is dropping the illusion. He has been putting a lot of meaning into something that is not real. His pill is an act of commitment, and it's also a "tracer" to find out where he really is. He started off with a desire to find out what's real, and then it transformed into a higher purpose to liberate others. It all started with what Morpheus called "a splinter in your brain." Like an itch you don't know how to scratch.

So I'm curious: do you find yourself in a similar place? Are you confused about what you want? Is there something big calling you but you don't know what it is? Do you know what it is but you're scared of it? Do you have a big desire, but you're just not sure what to do next?

This is your call to adventure.

What's Next?

I started by telling you about how this all came from watching a movie and wondering if it could be real. Now I'll end by asking you, what if you could be the director of the movie of your life?

129

What if you could drop the old story (by making your peace with it) and create a new one?

I'm not promising all your dreams will come true. I'm not promising you'll be 50 percent happier. What I'm offering you is awareness so that you can discover the truth and then focus on what you really want because energy flows in the direction of your intention.

Your life can change, one choice at a time. And after a while you'll start to notice...

- You're more honest with yourself and others.
- You're more clear and more productive
- You experience emotions rather than being ruled by them.
- You hold yourself to new standards.
- You have and enforce new boundaries.
- You have next level, high-quality problems.

Just remember this: While you can get a big aha moment or breakthrough, change stays by living in the body and your environment. Without a structure, life takes over. So I hope you'll accept our support and join our tribe.

Thank you for going on the journey of this book with me. I hope you'll continue it with a real experience.

Oh, and one last thing...

Be prepared to be surprised.

Afterword: Xpill, Shamanic Tool for Our Generation

When Robbe and Holly approached my partner, David, and I about being test subjects for Xpill, I thought it was a very innovative idea… but I have to be honest, I felt a little resistant. Yes, I had things I wanted to overcome, but I didn't need a pill. After all, I am a professional who helps people overcome issues everyday. I think Robbe must have sensed my block to the "play" aspect of his project and said something that immediately pulled me out of the overly analytical and carefully guised protest I was passively emitting.

He turned to Holly and said, *"Maybe she's not a candidate."*

Thankfully, I was shocked back into my natural state of curious exploration with Robbe's simple but effective reverse psychology tactic, and I started to play nice.

Over the next few weeks I had some rather profound experiences taking Xpill. I won't get into those now, but I will tell you what I wasn't expecting to discover.

As a therapist, I know that each person must be willing to do the work of scraping the depths of their subconscious to reprogram damaging beliefs into healthy subroutines. The

131

therapist uses "tools," not unlike the Xpill, to coax those nasty little false beliefs into the light where they can be processed and released.

As a lifetime student of theology and shamanism I also realized something very vital about these little purple pills.

They are little but very powerful shamanic tools for the new millennia.

Let me explain.

Historically, in tribal cultures certain symbols and rituals are given spiritual, even magical meanings that are maintained and reinforced over many generations by the communal psyche. This cultural relationship to symbols eases the work of the shaman by immediately bypassing the logical conscious mind to access the deep subconscious mind where the root of what ails you lies laughing devilishly in a corner.

We call this instilled meaning *symbolic penetration*. Here, the symbols are literal shamanic shortcuts into the deep subconscious that convey instant meaning, bring one into direct psychic contact with the divine, and/or act as tools to allow the inner mind to spit out the root of your problem in a big snotty mess right into your conscious world. This is where the shaman (therapist, priest, coach, or other guide) helps you through the process of release, forgiveness, and psychic reintegration.

Symbols are deeply imbued with relevance and power to a particular society. Take those symbols to another culture that has no connection to them and they will probably not experience the same immediate psychic rush of meaning.

Many crave a quick, magical fix to their issues and may be drawn to the romantic mysticism of a traditional shaman. Here, they directly confront their inner shadow world, facilitated by the use of whatever the particular shaman's "tools" are, and think that's all there is to it. The person who does not have a cultural relationship with the symbols used may, over time, lose much of the relevant healing process and discontinue the healing work altogether. The symbol used, although mystical in the moment, is not as deeply relevant and continuous in the psyche as it would be to a member of that culture.

The Shaman knows a powerful confrontation of the seeker's underworld, facilitated by the "tool," is only the first step to unraveling and processing what lies in the deep.

"The Pill" is a symbol that is already present in *our* culture and has long since penetrated our modern collective unconscious. The Xpill serves this purpose; it is a shamanic tool we are *already familiar with*. It is our shamanic rattle, rattling what is needed forward to be confronted and released. Even if our logical conscious minds protest, as mine did at first, our powerful subconscious minds will not let us run far from what we already know.

For my Xpill journey, I chose to resume working on my music. Music had been a big part of my life and a profession until my divorce in 2006, when I began my current career path. As I

133

worked though the blocks I thought were stopping me from resuming my practice and began actually practicing again, I was confronted with a reality I wasn't expecting. I had already redirected my creative energies into my current life in a new and more satisfying way, and no longer "needed" music in the way I thought I did. Now, free to allow music into my life in a more natural way, the urgent feeling that somehow I was being disloyal to my gift is gone.

The modern shaman must understand the relevance of the symbol they choose to invoke healing for the culture they engage with. Robbe and Holly, shamans of the new millennia, have brilliantly followed the shamanic tradition in a totally and culturally relevant manner. This little purple pill has magic, power, and meaning for us, whether we like it or not. Allow the work to be facilitated by the symbol; your subconscious mind knows what to do with it. Let it happen, let the process work. It is truly a shamanic method more time-proven and potent than you realize.

Heather Kim Rodriguez, PhD, DNH
October 31, 2016
Las Vegas, Nevada
ZenRoseGarden.com

So, now. What is it you want?

You can think about it.
You can look at your life and try to "figure it out."
You can toy with options.
You can ask friends.
But these are all ways to keep yourself from moving forward.

The more clarity you seek, the less you have.

The more you google, the more you read books, find experts, take programs, seek advice, then you're just creating a traffic jam of options in your head.

Deciding isn't a mental decision.
It's a physical act.

What's your Xpill?

www.Xpill.com

NOTES/PERSONAL INDEX

Page	Notes

NOTES/PERSONAL INDEX

Page	Notes

NOTES/PERSONAL INDEX

Page	Notes

www.ingramcontent.com/pod-product-compliance
Lightning Source LLC
Chambersburg PA
CBHW061146040426
42445CB00013B/1577